Intersectional Inequality

Intersectional Inequality

Race, Class, Test Scores, and Poverty

CHARLES C. RAGIN
AND PEER C. FISS

The University of Chicago Press
Chicago and London

The University of Chicago Press, Chicago 60637
The University of Chicago Press, Ltd., London
© 2017 by The University of Chicago
All rights reserved. Published 2017.
Printed in the United States of America

26 25 24 23 22 21 20 19 18 17   1 2 3 4 5

ISBN-13: 978-0-226-41437-9 (cloth)
ISBN-13: 978-0-226-41440-9 (paper)
ISBN-13: 978-0-226-41454-6 (e-book)
DOI: 10.7208/chicago/9780226414546.001.0001

Library of Congress Cataloging-in-Publication Data
Names: Ragin, Charles C., author. | Fiss, Peer C., author.
    Title: Intersectional inequality : race, class, test scores, and poverty / Charles C. Ragin and Peer C. Fiss.
    Description: Chicago ; London : The University of Chicago Press, 2017. | Includes bibliographical references and index.
    Identifiers: LCCN 2016023259 | ISBN 9780226414379 (cloth : alk. paper) | ISBN 9780226414409 (pbk. : alk. paper) | ISBN 9780226414546 (e-book)
    Subjects: LCSH: Equality. | Poverty—United States. | Race—Social aspects—United States. | Educational equalization—United States. | Equality—Research. | Social sciences—Methodology.
    Classification: LCC HM821 .R34 2017 | DDC 305—dc23 LC record available at https://lccn.loc.gov/2016023259

CONTENTS

ACKNOWLEDGMENTS

Perhaps more so than others, this book has been a work of patience. It started well back in the early 2000s and has been a steadfast companion ever since, sometimes taking center stage, and other times waiting in the wings until it reemerged. While the original goal of this book has in fact changed relatively little since it was first sketched, many other events took place in our lives during this journey. We both moved, more than once and primarily west until the Pacific stopped us. Two children were born, and two others grew into adulthood. Other books and articles were written and published, yet this one was still plodding along, awaiting its time. Now that this time has finally come, it will be missed for its companionship, although that does little to dampen the pleasure of seeing it finally emerge and take actual shape.

As is only natural, when a book has been developing for such a long time it is especially difficult to acknowledge everyone who has influenced the ideas presented here. Many friends and colleagues at a variety of institutions enriched this book with their thoughtful comments, encouragement, and their own patience. We most certainly will miss recognizing many who deserve our thanks, and for that we sincerely apologize. That being said, our appreciation goes to Camilla Borgna, Thomas Cook, Mary Driscoll, Jon Kvist, Susan Mayer, and Christopher Winship. Barry Cooper read the complete manuscript, offering many sharp insights and helpful observations. He deserves our special thanks. Ange-Marie Hancock forced us to clarify our thinking on intersectionality, and an anonymous reader at the University of Chicago Press thoughtfully challenged us to refine our arguments and analyses. Sean Davey provided programming expertise and turned loosely connected code into a coherent software package. The materials of this book have been presented, in various forms, in colloquia and talks at the

University of Arizona, the University of California, Berkeley, the University of California, Irvine, the University of Chicago, Indiana University, the University of Milan, the University of North Carolina, the University of Oslo, the University of Southern Denmark, Tilburg University, and the University of Zurich. We would also like to acknowledge Richard Arum, who provided data used in the analyses of Fischer et al.'s book *Inequality by Design* and graciously answered our questions. We also thank Doug Mitchell and Kyle Wagner for their help and enthusiastic support in getting this work to print.

Both of us are deeply grateful to our families and especially our spouses, Mary and Géraldine, who have shared companionship with this work, kept encouraging us, and nudged us over the finishing line. It may have been more than a nudge. They may not want much to do with this book anymore, but we would still like to dedicate it to them.

Introduction

Two features of social science that distinguish it from other ways of representing social phenomena are its explicit dialogue with theory and its commitment to systematic methodology (Ragin and Amoroso, 2011). The latter is especially important because methodology provides conventions both for constituting evidence and for crafting representations of social phenomena (i.e., "results") from evidence. When social research is conducted with the goal of contributing to policy debates, methodology is not a mere academic question, but also a political issue because different methodologies may produce fundamentally different representations of the same evidence (i.e., different "results" or "findings"). Representations can diverge sharply even when the definition of what constitutes relevant evidence (e.g., survey data) is held constant.

The central analytic focus of most policy-oriented social research today is the estimation of the "correct" effect size and the assessment of the relative importance of competing independent variables in multivariate analyses. For instance, a researcher might ask: "Which variable has the strongest impact on life chances: education, test scores, or family background?"[1] Framing multivariate analyses in terms of a competition between variables dovetails with everyday forms of ideological opposition. That is, there is a direct connection between conventional quantitative methodology and ideological debate because competing variables in multivariate analyses are

---

1. We use the term *test scores* in this work to refer to such tests as the Armed Forces Qualification Test (AFQT), championed by some (e.g., Herrnstein and Murray in *The Bell Curve*) as a test of general intelligence. While there are very good reasons to doubt the claim that these tests measure general intelligence, for the most part we avoid taking a position in this debate and simply use the generic term *test scores*.

usually linked to different ideological positions. This linking of variables and ideological positions is apparent in a number of policy debates, including the one generated by *The Bell Curve*, which spawned a controversy over the importance and use of so-called intelligence and school achievement tests as predictors of life chances.

The fact that conventional forms of multivariate analysis, on the one hand, and ideological opposition, on the other, are mutually reinforcing is unfortunate. Their link undermines the potential value of social research to policy discourse, especially in such politically charged arenas as education and social inequality. One consequence of this link is that researchers tend to focus almost exclusively on the competition between variables to determine their relative importance and fail to consider how different factors may work together and the different contexts that enable one cause versus another. A related consequence is that researchers frequently overlook the possibility that there may be several different paths to the same outcome, involving different combinations of causally relevant conditions. The relevant paths also may differ by other factors, for example, race and gender. The finding that test scores have a significant net effect on life chances, for example, does not help us understand how they have this effect, in what contexts, or in combination with what other conditions. A more textured understanding of the connection between test scores and life chances is possible, however, if the analyst is willing to abandon the competition between variables and focus instead on the diverse ways in which combinations of causal conditions and outcomes are linked.

In the chapters that follow we offer an alternative to the conventional approach to the analysis of policy-relevant social data. Instead of asking, "What is the net effect of each independent variable (e.g., test scores versus family background) on the outcome (e.g., avoiding poverty)?" we ask, "What *combinations* of causally relevant conditions are linked to the outcome?" In this view, causal conditions do not compete with each other; rather, they combine in different ways to produce the outcome. This alternate approach allows for the possibility that there may be many paths to the same outcome, and it does not force the incremental effect of each causal variable on the outcome (e.g., on the log odds of avoiding poverty) to be the same for each case. In essence, we propose and offer a diversity-oriented understanding of the connections between causal conditions and outcomes because it views cases *intersectionally*—in terms of the different ways they combine causally relevant conditions.

The diversity-oriented techniques we use are set-analytic in nature and build upon the case-oriented techniques first presented in *The Comparative*

Method (Ragin, 1987) and then extended in *Fuzzy-Set Social Science* (Ragin, 2000) and *Redesigning Social Inquiry* (Ragin, 2008). These works demonstrate how to identify the multiple paths to an outcome using set-analytic methods. By viewing cases intersectionally and causes conjuncturally, it is possible to allow for much greater diversity and heterogeneity, and researchers can address nuanced questions about causal conditions. For example, instead of asking, "What is the net impact of test scores on poverty status?" we can ask, "Under what conditions is there a connection between low test scores and experiencing poverty?" This nuanced question can be answered by examining the different paths to poverty and pinpointing those that include low test scores as part of the mix of causally relevant conditions. Nuanced findings, in turn, are more directly relevant to policy makers and policy discourse and may open up new avenues for moving beyond established positions, making set-analytic methods especially suitable for informing policy analysis (e.g. Rihoux and Grimm, 2006; Glaesser and Cooper, 2012a, 2012b; Hudson and Kühner, 2013).

Overview

To demonstrate the added value of intersectional methods, we reexamine evidence used in two well-known policy-relevant studies—*The Bell Curve* (Herrnstein and Murray, 1994) and *Inequality by Design* (Fischer et al., 1996). We focus on the controversy surrounding the predictors of poverty status because of the centrality of this question to current issues and trends in education and educational reform, and, in turn, the centrality of education to U.S. social and economic policy.

Chapter 1 presents our view of the essential features of social inequality and elaborates the methodological implications of that understanding. In a nutshell, we view social inequality in terms of overlapping and reinforcing advantages versus disadvantages, with a special focus on the different ways advantages and disadvantages are configured by race and gender. This view of social inequality calls for the use of analytic techniques that attend to the links between different *combinations* of advantages and disadvantages, on the one hand, and outcomes such as poverty, on the other.

Chapter 2 reviews the *Bell Curve* debate, focusing on the controversy regarding the impact of test scores on life chances. Of special importance to our argument is the challenge to the *Bell Curve* posed by Fischer et al.'s *Inequality by Design*. The contrast between these two works illustrates the specification dependence of estimates of net effects of test scores on poverty status. Herrnstein and Murray opt for lean specification, which yields a large net effect of test scores, while Fischer et al. specify an elaborate model, yielding a much smaller net effect of test scores. This entirely predictable difference underscores the limitations of the net effects approach to policy-relevant social research.

In chapter 3 we use logistic regression techniques to reproduce and evaluate the results of Fischer et al.'s analysis of the data from the National Longitudinal Survey of Youth (NLSY). After reproducing their results, we offer several corrections to their model and then evaluate it with respect to its predictive power—how well it assigns cases to the outcome *in-poverty* versus *not-in-poverty*. We then offer our own logistic regression model, which charts a middle path between the two approaches by using a moderate number of independent variables. These variables also provide the basis for the fuzzy sets we use in our set-analytic assessment of the NLSY data.

Chapter 4 details the construction of the fuzzy sets we use in the set-theoretic analyses we present in chapters 5–8. Fuzzy sets capture the degree of membership of cases in sets, with scores ranging from 0 to 1. Scores must be calibrated in a manner that is consistent with the conceptualization and labeling of the set in question (e.g., degree of membership in the set of respondents with high test scores). The fuzzy sets we create assess degree of membership in various respondent and family background characteristics. To ensure the robustness of our findings, we utilize multiple calibrations of key variables. For example, we calibrate separately degree of membership in the set of respondents with high-income parents and degree of membership in the set of respondents with low-income parents.

The *Bell Curve* focuses on the competition between two independent variables, family background and test scores. Chapter 5 addresses the *Bell Curve* directly, assessing the set-theoretic connections between family background—especially parental income—and test scores on the one hand, and poverty on the other. Our results reveal a distinct pattern of racial confounding that is hidden in standard correlational analysis. Specifically, advantages and avoiding poverty are linked in the white male and white female samples, while disadvantages and experiencing poverty are linked in the black male and black female samples. We find parallel patterns of results in our analysis of the impact of parental income and test scores on poverty and document a very high degree of set coincidence of these two conditions.

The examination of coinciding advantages versus disadvantages is expanded in chapter 6 to encompass other inequalities. Specifically, we examine the degree to which parental income, parental education, respondent's education, and respondent's test scores coincide, using multiple calibrations of these four conditions. We again show that the intersectionality of these inequalities has a distinctly racial pattern. We then move on to examine the degree to which these different coinciding advantages and disadvantages are linked to poverty and its avoidance. Because set-analytic assessment is inherently asymmetric, we are able to separate the analysis of advantages from the analysis of disadvantages and also the analysis of being in poverty from the analysis of avoiding poverty. Our findings demonstrate that whites more than blacks experience overlapping and reinforcing advantages, while blacks more than whites experience overlapping and reinforcing disadvantages.

Chapter 7 further refines this analysis by using truth table techniques to derive causal recipes for avoiding poverty. We perform these analyses separately for white and black males and females and also at different levels of consistency of poverty avoidance. Our analysis reveals a stark racial contrast: To achieve poverty avoidance levels comparable to whites, blacks must combine more advantages. Thus, our results reveal that blacks are doubly disadvantaged—they possess, on average, fewer advantages, yet more advantages are required of blacks in order to achieve the same consistency of poverty avoidance that whites experience.

Chapter 8 summarizes the main findings of chapters 5–7 and presents a truth table analysis of the size of the racial gap in consistency of poverty avoidance. The broad pattern we find is that the greater the number of disadvantages, the greater the racial gap in consistency scores for avoiding poverty. These findings complement our chapter 7 results and again underscore the importance of racial differences in addressing social inequality in the U.S. today. We conclude this final chapter by returning to the *Bell Curve* debate and sketching the implications of both our findings and our intersectional approach for the study of poverty and inequality.

ONE

When Inequalities Coincide

The Compound Nature of Social Inequality

Inequality is a key feature of human social organization—some would say it is *the* key feature. Inequality is praised by some as an engine of progress via the competition it spawns and condemned by others as a scourge, the source of countless social ills. One key aspect of inequality is that it pervades virtually all spheres of social life, from straightforward issues such as the distribution of income (who gets the high-paying jobs?) and education (who gets to stay in school longer and who gets to go to the best schools?) to more mundane things like parenting (who has more time to supervise and support their children and their education?) and focus (who has fewer anxieties about basic survival issues in their lives?).

In almost all known societies, inequalities coincide, compound, and reinforce. It is certainly not accidental that the people with the most income tend to have the best educations, live in the best neighborhoods, send their children to the best schools, take more vacations, have more time to supervise and socialize their children, have fewer demands on their attention, have greater personal security, can pay others to perform time-consuming manual tasks, and so on. These advantages are all connected, and they tend to support and reinforce each other. The most obvious example of a reinforcing link is the one between education and occupation, but there are other connections that are not so obvious, for instance between education and personal safety. Consider, for instance, children living in "rough" neighborhoods who face a daily challenge of navigating dangerous turf on their way to school. It takes a great deal of time, energy, and intellectual effort to accomplish things that would be considered completely routine and taken for granted in "good" neighborhoods. Children in rough neighborhoods would be much better off if they could pour all this "just-staying-safe" energy into their schoolwork. In short, these and other disadvantages often "cascade" (Lin and Harris, 2010: 3) in the sense that they tend to exacerbate other disadvantages.

The argument that advantages and disadvantages are cumulative in nature is, of course, not novel and has frequently been invoked as a key to understanding social inequality (e.g., Merton, 1968; Jencks and Mayer, 1990; Nolan and Whelan, 1999; DiPrete and Eirich, 2006). It is evident that inequalities reinforce each other at both ends of the continuum from poor to rich, resulting in a system of advantages and disadvantages that has profound implications for understanding social inequality (Lin and Harris, 2010). In our society, those in the middle strive to achieve the nexus of reinforcing advantages that comes with being at the top, and they desperately try to avoid the reinforcing disadvantages that push people toward the bottom (Pattillo-McCoy, 1999; Leicht and Fitzgerald, 2006). The bottom is a trap to be avoided at all costs; the top is a promised land commonly known as "having *really* made it." For many, however, fear of the dreaded bottom and the perilous strata of the middle that border it keeps pushing the definition of "having *really* made it" ever upward. While definitions shift, the fundamental truth remains that up and down the ladder of human social organization, hierarchies reinforce and reproduce each other. Of course, the fit between hierarchies is rarely perfect, and the strength of both the connections and the reinforcing mechanisms (at both the top and the bottom) varies by time and place. Nevertheless, the connections are durable (Tilly, 1999) and seemingly inevitable, as people everywhere do whatever they can to acquire, maintain, and reproduce advantage for themselves and their children.

Analytical Consequences

The fact that social inequalities coincide and reinforce has direct methodological implications, as variables that characterize the positions of individuals in social hierarchies tend to be correlated, sometimes very strongly. For example, there is a well-known and documented connection between years of education and occupational prestige, which is illustrated in figure 1.1, using data from the General Social Survey. As the figure shows, there is a clear upward trend to the plot—having more education is linked to occupations with higher prestige. Perhaps more striking than the well-documented upward trend, however, is the fact that the upper left triangle—almost half the area of the plot—is virtually devoid of cases. This section of the plot is for lower-education individuals with higher-prestige occupations. As

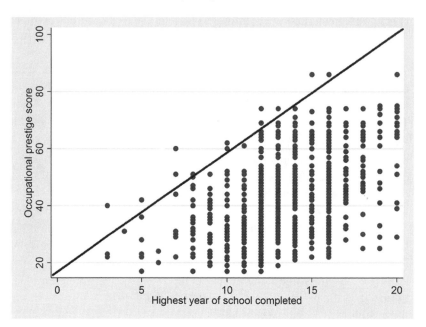

1.1. The relationship between education and occupational prestige.

the evidence in figure 1.1 indicates, low-education individuals are virtually barred from high-prestige occupations, suggesting in turn that spend-
ing many years in school is a virtual necessary condition for obtaining
a high prestige job. Notice also, however, that the lower right triangle of
the plot contains a considerable number of cases—indicating that high-
education individuals do not always obtain high-prestige jobs. Thus, the
triangular shape of the plot indicates that the connection between education and occupational prestige is both *correlational* (the upward drift) and
set-theoretic: people with high-prestige jobs constituting a subset of the people with high levels of education, suggesting that a high level of education
is *necessary but not sufficient* for a high prestige job.

The important point for now is that social inequalities (based upon education, income, occupational prestige, neighborhood, home ownership,
property values, school quality, race, ethnicity, and so on) tend to be strongly
linked in society and thus tend to be correlated as variables at the individual
level. Consequently, when social scientists study connections between different dimensions of social inequality, they are typically confronted with
the problem of confounded effects (i.e., multicollinearity). Take, for example, the well-known link between race and poverty—the rate of poverty is

considerably higher for blacks than for whites. How much of this difference in rates can be explained by the fact that blacks, on average, have less education than whites? How much of the difference can be explained by the fact that the average parental income (and parental education and parental property ownership and so on) is much higher for whites than blacks? Given that these explanatory factors tend to correlate with each other and also with the outcome, differences in "raw" rates can be misleading.

Accordingly, researchers have spent considerable effort teasing apart the unique or "net" effects of confounded explanatory variables. So far, the key tool for analyzing the effect of variables has been advanced multivariate regression techniques, which are commonly used to provide "corrected" estimates that take confounded inequalities into account by statistically controlling for the effects of correlated variables such as education, parental income, and so on when assessing the connection between variables like race and poverty. State-of-the-art multivariate techniques have been fine-tuned by social scientists and statisticians into powerful tools for the task of producing correct estimates of the effects of correlated inequalities that impact important life outcomes such as poverty.

Yet, given the overlapping nature of social inequalities, the Gordian knot of confounded variables is often difficult to unravel. For instance, consider recent debates on the importance of female-headed families in explaining rising income inequality. A significant body of regression-based studies have aimed to estimate the correct effect size, yet results remain inconclusive and estimates range from 11% to 41% (McLanahan and Percheski, 2008. Similarly, a large literature has examined the size of the welfare effect on family formation, yet the magnitudes of the estimated effects vary widely (e.g., Mofitt, 1998).

Generally, when social scientists seek to estimate the corrected effect of such causal factors as race or education or parental income, they focus on the variation in the outcome (e.g., poverty) that each of the competing variables explains *uniquely*. If the explanatory variables are strongly correlated with each other (and with the outcome), then each will have a relatively small net effect on the outcome. If, by contrast, they are only weakly correlated with each other (and, again, all are correlated with the outcome), then each will have a relatively larger net effect on the outcome.

Focusing on the unique contribution of each explanatory variable is a more promising approach when predictors are weakly correlated. In contrast, when the predictors are strongly correlated, the variation explained uniquely by each construct of interest becomes minor in comparison to the explained variation that is confounded, suggesting that it may be more promising to focus on the ways in which these explanatory factors overlap and intersect. Furthermore, if these predictors indeed compound and reinforce each other, then we might want to further explore the ways in which the predictors overlap.

Beyond Net Effects: Intersectionality

Estimating the net effects of variables that are correlated with each other is an important task, and, as previously noted, such analyses have the potential to uncover mechanisms that would otherwise be hidden to the unschooled observer. However, the core logic of the procedure—estimating each variable's separate, unique impact on an outcome—runs counter to social inequality's core nature, namely, that its various aspects and expressions are interconnected and reinforcing. In other words, the technology that social scientists have devised to untangle confounded effects (like respondent's education and parental income) are designed to neutralize, not capture, social inequality's essential underlying character. When a researcher estimates the net effect of education or race or some other variable on an important life outcome, the estimate that is derived is in fact *purged* of the effects of correlated inequalities. Yet an approach where education or any other variable connected to social inequality is assumed to have its own "independent" effect is not well suited to capture the coinciding nature of social inequalities that gives them their resilience and their power.

Consider an alternate approach to the analysis of social inequality, one that draws on the growing literature on "intersectionality." Emerging primarily from critical race studies in the late 1980s, the concept of intersectionality was used by Crenshaw (1989) as an analytical tool to denote "the various ways in which race and gender interact to shape the multiple dimensions of Black women's . . . experiences" (Crenshaw, 1991: 1244). Specifically, intersectionality "refers to the interaction between gender, race, and other categories of difference in individual lives, social practices, institutional arrangements, and cultural ideologies and the outcomes of these interactions in terms of power" (Davis, 2008: 68). Its analytical leverage stems from the fact that it shifts the focus from the separate effects of, for example, race and gender towards their combined and synergistic effects, thus emphasizing the multidimensionality of marginalized subjects' lived experience (Nash, 2008). The critical insight intersectionality offers is that characteristics such as race, gender, class, and so on operate as mutually constructed phenomena that shape social inequality (Collins, 2015).

While the original understanding of intersectionality was primarily oriented around notions of identity, the concept has since been broadened, and a number of debates have ensued (see, e.g., Davis, 2008; Walby et al., 2012). For our purposes, we want to retain the focus on intersectionality as an analytical tool for understanding the combinatorial nature of disadvantages while also extending it to apply to advantages. Our approach is most closely aligned with that of Hancock (2007a, 2007b, 2013), who sees intersectionality less as an area of substantive specialization but rather as a normative and empirical research paradigm that enables researchers to conceive of better research designs and data collection efforts based on attention to causal complexity (Hancock, 2007a). More concretely, intersectionality in practice means paying attention to analytic—though not necessarily statistical—interaction: "a transformative interactivity of effects" (Choo and Marx Ferree, 2010: 131).

The intersectionality approach carries several implications for policy analysis. First, its goal is to make the researcher attentive to the various and differing ways inequalities are experienced by social groups (e.g., Hankivsky and Cormier, 2011). Beyond this and perhaps even more importantly, intersectional policy analysis has to potential to improve the diagnosis of social inequality and to promulgate new approaches to alleviate its consequences. In focusing on the intersectional nature of inequality we agree with Hancock (2007b) who argues that "emphasizing the interaction between these factors will illuminate a comprehensive picture, providing the best chance for an effective diagnosis and ultimately an effective prescription."

Intersectionality in Practice

The combinatorial and interactive emphases of the intersectionality perspective carry significant methodological implications. First, the approach is fundamentally comparative and relational (McCall, 2005; Hancock, 2013; Collins, 2015), making it compatible with the comparative set-analytic methods we use here. Second, the approach requires a methodology that is interaction seeking (Choo and Marx Ferree, 2010); that is, it assumes combinations of conditions as the default analytical starting point. As Choo and Marx Ferree note, much of current quantitative methodology is not attentive to such concerns but instead emphasizes parsimonious models that work against "seeing or seeking complexity. Ingrained habits of reductionism, above and beyond any concern with data management issues, often drive conceptual analysis rather than the reverse" (2010: 146–147). In contrast, an approach that places intersectionality at its center has to move away from a focus on the net effects of "independent" variables understood in isolation from each other, and towards a relational approach that focuses on the different ways inequalities intersect.

From a conventional quantitative viewpoint, one could argue that intersecting inequalities are captured in a correlation matrix, which shows the bivariate correlations for all the variables included in a multivariate analysis. However, the issue is not the degree to which one variable is *correlated* with another across cases, but how multiple aspects of inequality are *jointly configured*, how they intersect, at the case level. What are the most common configurations? How strongly do different aspects of social inequality clump together at the top? How strongly do they coincide at the bottom? Knowing the different ways that inequality is configured is much more analytically incisive than knowing the degree to which different aspects of inequality correlate, with researchers looking at pairs of attributes, one pair at a time. A correlation matrix has a very limited ability to show, for example, whether or not advantages or disadvantages clump together, and if so, in what specific combinations. Nor does a correlation matrix easily show whether inequality is configured differently for whites and blacks or for males and females. The alternate way of thinking about inequality we suggest here—in terms of combinations of advantages versus disadvantages—shifts the focus from variables to kinds of cases (Ragin and Becker, 1992; Byrne and Ragin, 2009). Here, different configurations of inequality can be seen as constituting different kinds or types of cases. Instead of focusing on the unique effect of just one attribute, we see cases as configurations of intersecting attributes.

As a simple illustration of this idea of examining the different ways inequality is configured, consider the hypothetical data shown in table 1.1. The data illustrate different paths towards avoiding poverty. There are two causal conditions, both dichotomies—respondent has high test scores (yes/no) and respondent has middle-to-high income parents (yes/no). The outcome is also dichotomous—respondent successfully avoids poverty (yes/no). With two dichotomous causal conditions, there are four combinations of values, as shown in the table. In this hypothetical data set, however, there is a further issue—namely, there are no cases that combine the presence of high test scores with low-income parents. Such situations, we would suggest, are common, though certainly not as extreme as presented in table 1.1. In most nonexperimental research, we do not observe all logically possible combinations of conditions, a phenomenon known as limited diversity (Ragin, 1987).

Let us begin by taking the standard approach of comparing rates. Examining the two causal conditions of test scores and parental income one at a time, it is clear that having high test scores is more important. Respondents with high test scores stay out of poverty at a rate of 97%, while respondents

Table 1.1 Hypothetical data illustrating importance of configurations.

High test scores	Middle/high income parents	Proportion avoiding poverty	Number of cases
yes	yes	.97	100
yes	no	—	0
no	yes	.80	100
no	no	.79	100

lacking high test scores stay out of poverty at a rate of 79.5%, a 17.5 point difference. By contrast, respondents with middle/high income parents stay out of poverty at a rate of 88.5% (the average of rows one and three in the table), while respondents with low-income parents stay out of poverty at a rate of 79%, a 9.5 point difference. A logistic regression analysis of these data confirms the greater explanatory power of test scores. The net effect of having high test scores is positive and significant with an odds ratio of more than 8.0, while the net effect of parental income is not significant, with an odds ratio very close to 1.0 (i.e., no impact whatsoever). Thus, a conventional analysis of these data with its focus on net effects would lead to the conclusion that, when it comes to staying out of poverty, high test scores are important; parental income does not appear to play a significant role.

However, when we take an intersectional approach, it becomes clear from looking at the evidence in the table that this conclusion is not warranted. Consider asking a different question, using the same evidence: What conditions are linked to a very high rate of poverty avoidance? This time, instead of comparing test scores and parental income as "independent" variables, we now focus on the outcome of interest first. As the table shows, there is a single row with a high rate of poverty avoidance—the first. Cases in this row combine high test scores *and* middle-to-high-income parents. Viewed from this perspective, the evidence in the table does not support the argument that all that really matters is having high test scores regardless of parental income, given that those who are the best at avoiding poverty have not only high test scores but also middle-to-high-income parents. In other words, it is this specific *combination* of characteristics that provides sure-fire protection from poverty, not high test scores alone.

To prove a unique effect of test scores alone, we would need to examine the counterfactual that might be provided by cases in the second row: if individuals who combine high test scores with the absence of middle-to-high-income parents avoid poverty at roughly the same rate as individuals in the first row, we might be able to conclude with greater confidence that it is test scores alone that matter. However, there are no cases in the second row, indicating that we cannot rule out the view that it is the combination of test scores and income that allows individuals to avoid poverty at such a high rate.

The conventional net effects analysis of these data does not pay attention to this fact because of its privileging of parsimony. This feature is one of the core strengths of the approach, but it is important to understand that a strength also can be a weakness. If a causal condition has a trivial, nonsignificant effect in a multivariate analysis, the conventional practice is to interpret this as evidence that the causal condition is not relevant and either to drop it from the analysis or treat it as immaterial to the outcome. A configurational approach, by contrast, focuses on combinations of conditions and thus is less likely to relegate causal conditions to irrelevance. In some contexts a causal condition may contribute to the outcome in question; in others, it may not. Such contextually bound patterns can be ascertained only via fine-grained analysis of cases as combinations of conditions.

Intersectional Methods

In order to study how inequalities intersect, it is necessary to use analytic techniques that examine cases as *combinations* of aspects. Truth tables (Ragin, 1987, 2000, 2008) are especially useful for examining cases in terms of the different combinations of causally relevant conditions they display, making them a complementary tool for intersectionality research (Hancock, 2013). Truth tables list all logically possible combinations of values on relevant conditions and report the number of cases exhibiting each combination. With four conditions, there are 16 logically possible combinations of conditions; with five, there are 32 combinations; with six, 64; and so on. Consider, for illustration, table 1.2, which shows the 16 logically possible combinations of four conditions linked to avoiding poverty: *not-low-income-parents*, *educated-parents*, *educated-respondent*, and *not-low-test-scores*.[1] To facilitate the analysis, combinations of conditions are listed separately for black males and white males.

The rows of the two truth tables shown in table 1.2 are sorted so that the most common combination is listed first; the second most common is listed second; and so on. The last column shows the cumulative proportion of cases. Table 1.2 shows clearly that these individual-level attributes are strikingly "lumpy" in their distribution at the case level. That is, a small

---

1. Details regarding the construction of these sets are provided in chapter 4.

Table 1.2 **Using truth tables to study cases as configurations.**

Rank	Not-low parental income	Educated parent	Educated respondent	Not-low test score	Frequency	Cumulative proportion
White males						
1	1	1	1	1	927	.685144
2	1	0	1	1	79	.743533
3	0	1	1	1	76	.799704
4	1	1	1	0	65	.847746
5	1	1	0	1	33	.872136
6	0	0	0	0	32	.895787
7	0	0	1	1	31	.918699
8	1	0	1	0	21	.93422
9	1	0	0	0	20	.949002
10	1	1	0	0	17	.961567
11	0	1	0	0	15	.972653
12	1	0	0	1	11	.980783
13	0	0	1	0	11	.988914
14	0	1	1	0	9	.995565
15	0	0	0	1	4	.998522
16	0	1	0	1	2	1
Black males						
1	1	1	1	1	144	.199723
2	0	0	1	0	104	.343967
3	0	1	1	0	82	.457698
4	0	1	1	1	80	.568655
5	1	1	1	0	65	.658807
6	0	0	0	0	54	.733703
7	0	0	1	1	53	.807212
8	1	0	1	1	32	.851595
9	1	0	1	0	28	.89043
10	0	1	0	0	28	.929265
11	1	1	0	0	17	.952843
12	1	0	0	0	16	.975035
13	0	1	0	1	8	.98613
14	1	1	0	1	6	.994452
15	0	0	0	1	3	.998613
16	1	0	0	1	1	1

number of combinations are very common, and most combinations are relatively rare. Consider the white male distribution. Even though there are 16 logically possible combinations of the four attributes, the three most common combinations capture 80% of the cases, and the seven most common capture nearly all of the cases (92%). The pattern is striking, with the bottom nine combinations of conditions (i.e., more than half) together embracing only 8% of cases. The black male distribution is not nearly as lumpy, but still far from uniform. The seven most common combinations capture 81% of the cases, and the ten most common capture 93%. The remaining six combinations together embrace only 7% of the cases.

There are important differences not only in the distribution of respondents across combinations, but also in the composition of the most common combinations. For example, the most common white male combination brings together all four advantages. This single combination captures an impressive 68.5% of the white males. While this combination is also the most common among black males, it embraces only about 20% of these respondents, less than a third of the figure for white males. The second most common white male combination brings together three advantages. By contrast, this combination is the eighth most common black male combination. The second most common black male combination includes three disadvantages and embraces about 14% of black males; this same combination ranks thirteenth for white males, embracing less than 1% of the respondents. Finally, while the combination of four disadvantages is the sixth most common for both white males and black males, it embraces 8% of the black males but only 2% of white males.

It is important to consider the social consequences of these racial differences. Hypothetically, when an employer is approached by a white male applicant, there is a very good chance that the applicant is fully advantaged, and more often than not, the employer would not be mistaken to infer these advantages for all white male applicants. The picture is very different for black males. Approached by a black male applicant, the employer would be wrong most of the time to make the same positive attributions. It is almost as likely that the black male applicant has three of four disadvantages (the second most common black male combination).

Another way to compare the results for black and white males in table 1.2 is in terms of the patterns of 1s and 0s for the four conditions. A pattern of 1s across the four conditions indicates the presence of all four advantages combined (all four set membership scores are greater than .5); a pattern of 0s across these four conditions indicates the combined absence of these four advantages (all four set membership scores are less than .5). As noted previously, the most common white male and black male configuration is, in fact, the combination of four advantages. For white males, the next four combinations display three advantages and one disadvantage (i.e., all possible combinations of three advantages and one disadvantage). However, for black males, these same combinations rank fourth, fifth, eighth, and fourteenth, again demonstrating the racial skew of advantages.

Establishing the different ways social inequalities are configured is an important first step. The next step is to assess the consequences of these different configurations. For example, a researcher might want to ascertain the different combinations of background conditions linked to avoiding poverty. Do these combinations differ by race? Do they differ by gender? In chapters 4–8 we model the structure of the evidence presented in truth tables by applying logic minimization algorithms to the data they summarize. These models of the logical structure of the evidence show the different combinations of conditions linked to the outcome in question (e.g., avoiding poverty). It is possible, in turn, to view these different combinations as causal "recipes" for the outcome and to interrogate them further. For example, by examining the different recipes in which a particular condition is found (e.g., "not-low test scores"), the researcher can ascertain the contexts that enable a specific causal condition. Thus, using our approach it is possible to go beyond the assessment of net effects ("What is the net effect of test scores on the odds of staying out of poverty?") and address questions about enabling circumstances ("Under what conditions is having not-low test scores linked to staying out of poverty?").

The analyses presented in this chapter are not definitive; they are offered simply as examples of the nature of the methods and modes of argumentation presented in this work. Our key position is that social inequality is best examined (and understood) intersectionally, especially in terms of the different ways it is configured by race and gender. Instead of trying to neutralize inequality's essential combinatorial nature, which is the core logic of net effects approaches, we attempt to capitalize on it. To accomplish this, we use techniques that take as their starting point the different combinations of causally relevant conditions linked to an outcome, as illustrated in table 1.2.

Intersectional Analysis versus Interaction Analysis

A statistician at this point might object that, in some respects, our approach is comparable to estimating a saturated interaction model. After all, a truth table lists all logically possible combinations of causal conditions, which is roughly parallel to examining all possible statistical interactions among the causal variables. There are important differences between what we do, however, and the examination of statistical interaction.

First, it is important to note that saturated interaction models are not only quite demanding to compute (usually due to data limitations), but they are also very difficult to decipher and interpret. Interaction terms can be understood only in the context of the entire equation in which they appear; the more complex the interaction model, the more difficult it is to decipher the results.

Second, to overcome these limitations of evaluating interactions, it is common practice to test higher-order interactions against the lower-order interactions that are contained within the higher-order interaction. For example, a researcher might test a three-way interaction (A*B*C) against the three two-way interactions that are contained within it (A*B, A*C, and B*C). Does the higher-order interaction produce an increment to explained variation in the outcome, beyond what is captured by the lower-order terms (and by the "main effects")? This is a useful practice because most researchers favor parsimony over complexity, and additive equations (i.e., equations without interaction terms altogether) are the simplest to interpret. However, this bias toward parsimony and simplicity runs counter to the goal of looking at the ways that inequalities overlap—how social inequality is configured by race and gender. In short, the difficulty of analyzing complex statistical interaction tends to bias research away from understanding inequality in an intersectional manner.

Third, multicollinearity among related interaction terms in a saturated model is usually extreme, which in turn has a noxious and often lethal impact on the equation as a whole. Small empirical differences can spawn impressive-looking interaction effects via suppression and other data issues. Furthermore, when multicollinearity is severe, as is usually the case when higher-order interaction terms are examined, many different subsets of interaction terms will fit the evidence equally well—deciding which ones to trust becomes a rather difficult task.

Fourth, and most important of all from our viewpoint, is the fact that our approach is explicitly *set-theoretic*. That is, we are more concerned with connections that are uniform or close to uniform than with connections that reflect differences in tendencies. The outcome code in our truth table analyses are set-theoretic measures indexing the degree to which cases with each combination of conditions constitute a subset of instances of the outcome (e.g., how consistently a combination is linked to avoiding poverty). Of special interest from a set-analytic viewpoint are those combinations registering very high consistency scores, for cases with these combinations of attributes are the closest to being free of poverty. The goal of the analysis is to identify the different combinations of causally relevant conditions linked to this outcome. In other words, our aim is not to assess the incremental effects of various conditions (or even their combinations via interaction terms) on the log odds or probability of the outcome, as in a conventional quantitative analysis, but to identify the combinations of conditions consistently linked to the outcome. While a correlational analysis is focused on tendencies, our set-analytic approach is focused on direct connections between membership in causal conditions and outcomes.

Conclusion

Social inequalities tend to be cumulative and thus require an approach that acknowledges their intersectional nature. Yet the dominant methodological tools for the study of inequality are not well aligned with this feature. To be sure, net effects analyses, with or without allowances for statistical interaction, are very powerful and precise, and have contributed a great deal to our understanding of complex social phenomena. Yet their strength also becomes a weakness when the object is not to isolate unique contributions but to understand an outcome as the result of intersecting and reinforcing causes. Our goal in this work is not to supplant correlational techniques, but to complement them with an intersectional view of social inequality.

To demonstrate the utility of our approach, we first present conventional "net effects" analyses of the evidence (chapter 3) and then recast these analyses as intersectional analyses using fuzzy sets and truth tables (chapters 4–8). We show that it is possible to transcend debates about the relative importance of causal variables (e.g., the debate about which is more important, family background or test scores) and focus instead on causal recipes and the contexts that enable or disable specific connections. These different circumstances can be established through direct examination of the combinations of causal conditions consistently linked to outcomes.

TWO

Policy Context: Test Scores and Life Chances

Poverty remains one of the most pressing social problems of our time. In fact, the official poverty rate in the United States increased from 12.5% in 2007 to 15.0% in 2012 (Varner, Mattingly and Grusky, 2014). Taking a historical perspective, the U.S. poverty rate for 2012 is about 4 percentage points higher than the poverty rate in the early 1970s (Danziger and Wimer, 2014). As Varner et al. note, "The current poverty rates for the full population and for children rank among the very worst over the 13 years since 2000" (2014: 4). This increase in poverty is part of larger trend of growing inequality in the U.S. that began in the late 1960s to early 1970s, but has increased in pace since the 1980s (McCall and Percheski, 2010; Neckerman and Torche, 2007; Thompson and Smeeding, 2014). Income inequality is high in the U.S. not only in historical perspective, but also in an international perspective. Disposable cash income was more unequally distributed in the U.S. than in 29 of 32 other rich or middle-income countries (McCall and Percheski, 2010). Overall, the available data suggest "a broadly deteriorating poverty and inequality landscape" (Varner et al., 2014: 6).

Not surprisingly, poverty and its reduction continue to be core concerns of public policy. Understanding the reasons why some people end up in poverty while others do not has important policy implications, and the literature on the social inequality/social policy nexus is vast and multidisciplinary. Researchers with backgrounds in economics, political science, sociology, and psychology, among others, have all weighed in on the complex and interacting causes that make poverty such an intractable and persistent social ill. Furthermore, since the 1980s new longitudinal data sets and sophisticated quantitative estimation techniques have become available, and the statistical modeling of the causes of poverty has become considerably more nuanced and refined. Data sets such as the Panel Study of Income Dynamics (PSID) and the National Longitudinal Survey of Youth (NLSY) have been used extensively to assess the causes of poverty, and these data sets have been worked and reworked by a considerable number of researchers (see reviews by Corcoran, 1995; Lichter, 1997; Small and Newman, 2001). The debate over the causes of poverty provides a useful context for demonstrating how our intersectional approach to inequality provides new insight into longstanding issues.

Within the debate over the causes of poverty, there are few works that have created as much controversy as *The Bell Curve*, published in 1994. Authored by Richard Herrnstein and Charles Murray, the book had a much bigger impact on public debate than most other social policy publications. It gained several hundred thousand readers within a matter of months and appeared on the front covers of both *Newsweek* and *The New York Times Book Review*. Critics described it as "the most incendiary piece of social science to appear in the last decade or more" (Fraser, 1995:1) and "perhaps the most reviewed book in the social sciences" (Levine and Painter, 1998:1). Within the span of a year, two collections of essays on *The Bell Curve* were published (Fraser, 1995; Jacoby, Glauberman and Herrnstein, 1995), and within another two years a number of books emerged that aimed to make the case against Herrnstein and Murray's findings, using the same NLSY data (Fischer et al., 1996; Kincheloe, Steinberg and Gresson, 1996; Devlin, 1997).

The critiques of *The Bell Curve* were varied, and it is not our goal to reproduce the spectrum of arguments appearing in this debate. In particular, we will mostly not examine works that address ethical or political issues, but will focus instead on works that critique *The Bell Curve* from a methodological point of view—as in some way procedurally flawed or technically inadequate. In doing so, we will pay special attention to the response formulated by Fischer et al. in *Inequality by Design* (1996). In many respects, the analyses by Herrnstein and Murray and Fischer et al. present two ends of a single continuum, and we will contrast the "simple picture" strategy of Herrnstein and Murray with the "everything but the kitchen sink" approach of Fischer et al. From an intersectional perspective, neither approach is satisfactory, as both suffer from a focus on net effects and from the restrictive assumptions built into their common analytic technique, logistic regression. Essentially, in both authors' analyses, variables compete to explain variation in the outcome variable, and the goal of the analysis is to estimate the unique contribution of each independent variable across all cases. In *The Bell Curve*, the independent variables are few and the results simple. The test score variable wins the competition to explain variation in the odds of experiencing/avoiding poverty. In *Inequality by Design*, by contrast, the variables are many and the results complex. The effect of the test score variable withers in the face of a battery of competing variables. While their results suggest more complex relationships, the models employed by Fischer et al. face challenges teasing apart the complex links between a variety of individual-level characteristics, such as household formation decisions, and the odds of avoiding poverty.

In this chapter, we first briefly summarize the *Bell Curve* debate and the different lines of attack on Herrnstein and Murray's findings. We then step back and examine more closely the merits of this debate itself, especially how it is constrained by the analytic methods that researchers used.

The Persistence of the Black-White Test Score Gap

At the heart of Herrnstein and Murray's argument lies the fact that, on a number of tests purported to measure scholastic ability, blacks score about one standard deviation lower than whites (Jencks and Phillips, 1998). Both sides of the debate—liberal and conservative—usually agree on the existence of this gap, but diverge regarding its meaning and causes. Traditionally, those on the liberal side have blamed the test score gap on the effects of causes such as racial segregation, black poverty, inadequate schools in minority neighborhoods, and others. By contrast, those on the conservative side have invoked differences in family composition (especially the scarcity of two-parent families), a "culture of poverty," and—probably most controversially—genetic differences between blacks and whites.

For obvious reasons, the claim that the black-white test score gap has genetic rather than environmental causes has inflamed a heated debate. While a number of studies using data on adopted and mixed-race children suggest the link between test scores and genes would appear to be tentative at best (Nisbett, 1998), the issue continues to figure into the test score debate (e.g., Lahn and Ebenstein, 2009). One reason for this is that pure environmental explanations have their own difficulties. Blacks tend to score lower than whites at every socioeconomic level, making it difficult to argue for the influence of socioeconomic status alone. Furthermore, even when biological siblings are raised in the same family, their test scores rarely have a correlation greater than .5 (Jencks and Phillips, 1998), which suggests that test scores are not simply a proxy for family background. Against this background, we now turn to the various responses to Herrnstein and Murray's claims that test scores are a key predictor of life outcomes such as poverty.

The Test Score Controversy

Most critiques of Herrnstein and Murray's use of test scores as a measure of intelligence relate to one of two issues: (1) Do test scores capture a single general intelligence factor that explains social outcomes? And (2) is this "intelligence factor" unchanging (i.e., more or less fixed at birth) or subject to environmental influences? In terms of the data in question, Herrnstein and Murray derive their test scores from the Armed Forces Qualification Test (AFQT), a paper-and-pencil test that is part of the larger Armed Services Vocational Aptitude Battery (ASVAB). The AFQT is the primary screening device used by the U.S. armed forces to determine eligibility for military service. It combines a subject's score on four ASVAB subtests: arithmetic reasoning, mathematics knowledge, paragraph comprehension, and word knowledge. After calculating the g-loadings of these four subtests, Herrnstein and Murray state that the AFQT is "one of the most highly g-loaded tests in use" (1994: 607) and thus provides an especially good measure of intelligence.

In contrast to this claim, several authors have suggested that AFQT scores do not primarily measure one general factor of cognitive ability (e.g., Cawley et al., 1997). After a reanalysis of the NLSY data, these authors conclude that g is not one-dimensional, and that "not much should be made of the fact that g explains a majority of the covariance across test scores; this is an artifact of linear correlation analysis, not intelligence" (1997:180). These authors' principal components analysis of AFQT scores indicates the existence of several components apart from g, and that these other components account for as much as 50% of the variance in test scores. Furthermore, Cawley et al. find that g explains very little of the variance in wages when compared to education, family background, and region of residence, and that returns to g differ significantly across race and gender, a finding that contradicts Herrnstein and Murray's claim that racial differences disappear when controlling for age, test scores, and gender (Herrnstein and Murray, 1994: 325–326).

AFQT scores extracted from the NLSY data may be problematic as measures of "intelligence" for other reasons. In examining the bottom end of the AFQT distribution, Fischer et al. report that, by conventional standards, the bottom 5% of respondents in the NLSY sample would be classified as mentally retarded (1996: 65–66). However, after comparing the test scores with the interviewer ratings for retardation, Fischer et al. find that test scores and these evaluations often do not agree. Using this evidence, Fischer et al.

suggest another explanation, which is that at least some of the respondents in the bottom 5% were "screw-ups." That is, these respondents either rejected the test itself or did not bother to complete it properly. Fischer et al. offer two pieces of evidence to support this argument: First, some of the low scorers had scored at or above average in previous school-given aptitude tests. Second, a number of respondents scored well below chance, particularly in the last test section, suggesting that they did not complete the test and that their low scores are due to this factor rather than to inferior mental abilities.

Regarding the second issue—whether test scores measure innate, unchanging ability or whether they are formed in response to environmental influences—the findings of Herrnstein and Murray again have been strongly contested. In *The Bell Curve*, Herrnstein and Murray present evidence that education has little or no effect on test scores. In a reanalysis of the NLSY data, Fischer et al. (1996) find that age only weakly correlates with AFQT scores, while years of education and whether the test taker had been in an academic track showed much higher correlations, leading them to argue that the AFQT is really a test of schooling, not of native intelligence. Against the reverse claim, that students with high test scores will be more likely to stay in school and to get into academic programs, they invoke the finding that AFQT scores are more highly correlated with number of years in school *before* taking the test ($r = .54$) than with the number of years *after* taking the test ($r = .33$), thus making the AFQT scores better "predictors" of past schooling than future schooling.

The issue of whether education can increase test scores is also taken up by Winship and Korenman (1997). These authors find that, after correcting technical errors in Herrnstein and Murray's analyses, the model reveals an estimated increase of 2.5 points of IQ per year of education. This effect is more than double that found by Herrnstein and Murray. While no single number for the effect of education on test scores emerges, the authors argue that the "best guess" is somewhere between 2 and 4 points of IQ per year of education, which is substantially more than what Herrnstein and Murray found, indicating an effect of schooling on test scores. In further analyses comparing the effects of test scores versus schooling on income, Winship and Korenman conclude that the effect of education is about half of that of test scores when both are standardized. Taken together, these findings suggest that, in contrast to the finding of Herrnstein and Murray, there is in fact a substantial payoff to staying in school. In turn, these findings support more educational investment, a claim that goes against the *Bell Curve* thesis that test scores are innate and unchanging.

These findings suggest that Herrnstein and Murray's claims about AFQT scores—that they accurately measure a single general factor of cognitive ability that is largely stable over the life course—are questionable. In our own analysis of the role of test score in determining life outcomes such as poverty, we will remain largely agnostic regarding what it is these test scores actually measure. AFQT scores were originally designed to measure one capacity: suitability for military jobs. This trait may be somewhat related to intelligence, but not intelligence alone, and the Armed Forces themselves explicitly stated that aptitude tests such as the AFQT should not be confused with intelligence tests (U.S. Senate Committee on Armed Services, March 10, 1980). We essentially take the same view and will in the following treat test scores as aptitude scores for military jobs.

Omitted Variables

Another and perhaps even more important criticism of Herrnstein and Murray's analyses is the charge that these analyses omit a number of important variables that, if included, would significantly alter the conclusions of the book. For instance, several authors have argued that Herrnstein and Murray fail to elucidate important differences in the relationship between race and earnings because they do not control for gender differences in their analyses. Regarding such gender differences, Cavallo et al. (1997) find that the earnings of black males with average characteristics are somewhat lower than those of comparable white males, while the earnings of black females are somewhat higher than those of comparable white females. Cavallo et al. therefore argue that when males and females are grouped together, these differences offset each other and the racial earnings gap is obscured. In their own analyses of the NLSY, Cavallo et al. show what they claim are substantial racial earnings differentials, even after controlling for AFQT.

Other authors such as Fischer et al. (1996) have suggested that female respondents in the NLSY were far more likely to be poor than male respondents, and that respondents with children were also much more likely to be poor than childless respondents. Accordingly, these authors claim that Herrnstein and Murray, by not controlling for these predictors, overstate the importance of test scores.

Comparable arguments have been made regarding environmental influences and the social background of respondents, both of which might significantly influence a number of outcomes addressed by Herrnstein and Murray. For example, in examining the link between intelligence and criminal behavior, Manolakes (1997) suggests that Herrnstein and Murray's measure of socioeconomic status omits a number of indicators of the social environment that have been shown to influence criminality, such as type of environment (rural vs. urban), racial categories (Herrnstein and Murray restrict their analysis of crime to white males), and statistical interactions among these variables. Her findings suggest that after including these variables, socioeconomic status (SES) has a significant effect on crime, although the effect may only be of about the same magnitude as that of test scores. Along the same lines, Phillips et al. (1998) argue that SES as measured by Herrnstein and Murray is too narrow to serve as an indicator of environmental influences. In their own analyses that include additional environmental factors such as grandparents' educational attainment, mother's and children's household size, and parenting practices, the authors find that blacks are much more disadvantaged than suggested by analyses using the more restricted unidimensional measure favored by Herrnstein and Murray. According to these authors, such environmental differences account for more than half the test score gap between black and white five- and six-year-olds.

Perhaps the most extensive attempt to deal with Herrnstein and Murray's omitted variable bias is offered by Fischer et al. (1996). They include a considerable number of additional measures of respondents' individual characteristics and social background, as well as measures of the respondent's community and educational environment, such as whether the respondent lived in a rural or urban area and the percentage of disadvantaged students and dropouts at the respondent's high school. After incorporating an array of additional variables into their statistical model, Fischer et al. conclude that the *Bell Curve* model is much too simplistic and that their own more complex analyses perform much better in predicting respondents' life outcomes.

The Focus on Effect Sizes

As has become evident, the central features of the *Bell Curve* debate have been the argument that the AFQT is at best a doubtful measure of intelligence and the charge that the models presented by Herrnstein and Murray wrongly exclude a number of important variables and thus present a distorted picture, giving far too much weight to test scores as a predictor of life outcomes. While these are important issues, we turn now to examine what we consider a problematic aspect of the *Bell Curve* debate, namely its focus on net effects and the unique contribution of various predictors. This focus on net effects is especially evident in the various analyses of what predicts earnings and poverty. Even a casual observer of the debate over *The Bell*

Curve's findings is struck by the willingness of scholars on both sides of the debate to attach precise values to the estimates of the effects of different predictors. In taking issue with this focus on effect sizes, we suggest that much of the debate over the exact contribution of different variables amounts to skating on very thin ice. We first consider some examples of this focus on effect sizes, drawn directly from the debate.

For instance, consider the various analyses examining the effects of test scores and education on earnings. Using earnings as an outcome variable is especially attractive because it allows direct quantification of the dollar value of being white or of obtaining an additional year of education. In these analyses, results are packaged in a meaningful metric—the dollar returns to a change in the value of an independent variable. For example, in commenting on the need for gender controls in examining the earnings gap between blacks and whites, Cavallo et al. (1997:201) state:

> The earnings gap for "average" males is a $1,532 advantage for white males. This is a nearly 20-fold increase when compared with the [results for both males and females together]. Notice, again, that the earnings differential grows with age to a $5,136 earnings advantage for average white males at age 32.

These findings, the authors argue, are clearly inconsistent with Herrnstein and Murray's finding of no racial discrimination. In continuing their analysis for females, Cavallo et al. find the reverse pattern, where average black females earn $2,833 more than white females; at age 32 the gap in favor of black females is $4,275. This dramatic evidence of racial differences in earnings is obscured when males and females are pooled in the same analysis (1997:202).

A fairly precise calculation is also offered by Winship and Korenman, who compare the effects of intelligence and education on earnings. Citing Dickens et al. (1997), the authors place Herrnstein and Murray's most conservative estimates of the benefits of a single point of IQ at an additional $232 per year in earnings. In contrast, the benefits of an additional year of education appear somewhat larger—Winship and Korenman place their preferred estimate from a year of schooling at $626, an estimate that suggests a substantial monetary payoff (1997:232).

Further interpretations regarding coefficients are also offered by Fischer et al. in their analysis of gender effects on the probability of being in poverty. According to their models, when holding the AFQT and the other factors constant, "a women's parents would have had to have earned $63,000 more than the parents of an otherwise similar young man for her to have a risk of poverty as low as his" (1996: 88–89).

Critics of the *Bell Curve* have also focused on the relative importance of AFQT scores compared to other variables. Indeed, this controversy is the epicenter of the debate. For example, in examining the relative contribution of human capital measures such as education, job tenure, and work experience, Cawley et al. (1997:189–190) find that "if ability is the only regressor included, ability contributes between 0.118 and 0.174 to R^2. When we control for human capital measures, the marginal increase in R^2 due to ability falls to between 0.034 and 0.011." The authors therefore conclude that Herrnstein and Murray "dramatically overstate" the amount of variation that is uniquely explained by cognitive ability. A similar evaluation is offered by Fischer et al., who find that a respondent's background was just as important as AFQT score in predicting poverty. From this finding, they infer that social environment during childhood "matters statistically at least as much as do the test scores that purportedly measure intelligence. . . . The key finding of *The Bell Curve* turns out to be an artifact of its method" (1996: 85–86).

Placing Effect Sizes in Context

While we agree with these critics that Herrnstein and Murray's models lack a number of important variables—factors that would add much to our understanding of such outcomes as poverty, crime, and teenage pregnancy—we are somewhat less comfortable with the focus of the debate on the exact sizes of the absolute and relative contributions of these variables. The reasons for this discomfort stem from several sources.

Consider, for example, the fact that psychometric researchers have long debated the utility of using regression weights for purposes of prediction, and some have favored alternate weighting systems that pay less attention to the size of the regression coefficients and more attention to the predictive power of the model. Alan Gross (1981) describes the situation for which these different weighting systems were developed. Suppose a researcher is given the problem of developing a statistical model for predicting an outcome from a set of independent variables. The outcome of interest could be, for example, success in graduate school (Wiggins and Kohen, 1971). The traditional approach to this problem is to collect data for a sample of first-year graduate students and to compute weights for a number of predictor variables based upon ordinary least squares regression. To predict the outcome in a future sample of students, the researcher would then simply apply the first sample's regression weights to the second sample's data. The accuracy of the predicted outcomes can be measured as the correlation between the predicted and the actual scores of the second sample. In the psychometric literature, this correlation is known as the cross validity of the first sample regression weights (Gross, 1981).

The situation gets more difficult when the number of predictor variables is large, especially in relation to the sample size, since regression analysis is known to suffer from large sampling errors under such conditions. In such a situation, the estimated weights may in fact be very unstable, and a variety of regression solutions may exist that can differ greatly from one another but can all fit the evidence more or less equally well (Wainer, 1976; 1978). If that is the case, then just how one estimates the regression coefficients "don't make no nevermind" (Wainer, 1976), and even solutions using equal weights or weights that were randomly chosen except for sign may perform remarkably well in predicting the outcome of interest (Dawes, 1978; Wainer, 1978).

The main insight from this literature is that, while regression analysis may give us the best estimates of the actual coefficient size for large samples, there may still exist a vast array of almost equally good solutions, and even small perturbations in the data may yield very large changes in the estimated regression weights (Wainer, 1978). The implication of this is summed up by Wainer (1978: 271) as follows:

> In many situations involving real behavioral data, there can be great variability among the regression weights of a linear model without serious decrement in mean square error. When this occurs it is very hazardous to make inferences about the relative size of individual regression weights.

Given this insight, it appears to us that too much attention has been accorded to the exact sizes of regression coefficients in the *Bell Curve* debate. While it is indeed possible to say something about the sign and significance of different predictor variables, we believe that the findings of researchers on both sides of the test score debate should be treated with more caution. This is particularly true for the role of test scores, which has been at the center of the debate. Test scores certainly contribute to the explanation of outcomes such as poverty, but the exact amount of variance explained by them remains a subject that, in our opinion, should be treated with more caution.

Our concern about the interpretation of coefficients appearing in regression models is reinforced by the fact that all estimated effects, including those that purport to be *precise*, are completely specification dependent. As is well known to researchers using quantitative methods, the estimate of an independent variable's effect is powerfully swayed by its correlations with competing variables. Limit the number of correlated competitors and a chosen variable may have a substantial effect on the outcome; pile them on, and its net effect may be reduced to nil. The specification dependence of the estimation of net effects is well known, which explains why quantitative researchers are thoroughly schooled in the importance of "correct" specification. However, correct specification is deeply dependent on both strong theory and broad substantive knowledge, both of which are often lacking in social research. Many social scientific debates about "the facts of the matter" degenerate into irresolvable disagreements about specification decisions, which in the end seem to be based in part on researchers' habits and personal preferences.

The importance of model specification is apparent in the contrasts between the quantitative analyses published by Herrnstein and Murray in *The Bell Curve* and those published by Fischer et al. in *Inequality by Design*. We turn next to a more detailed examination of these contrasts and bring home our argument that the key problem is not the "specification gap" separating these two works, but their common reliance on techniques designed to assess the net effects of "independent" variables. In subsequent chapters, we make the case for using techniques designed to assess the different ways that social inequality is configured and present an alternate analysis of the NLSY data.

The Bell Curve versus *Inequality by Design*

In their analysis of poverty, Herrnstein and Murray use a spare and undemanding logistic regression model that assesses the effects of only three independent variables: test scores, age, and "socioeconomic status" (an index based on the respondent's parental income, education, and occupational status).[1] When comparing the ability of these three variables to explain variation in the outcome of interest, the main finding of Herrnstein and Murray is that the test score variable is a stronger predictor of poverty than either age or socioeconomic background. From this finding, the authors draw their conclusion that, all else being equal, it is better to be born smart than to be born rich (Herrnstein and Murray, 1994:127).

---

1. All of Herrnstein and Murray's analyses with poverty as the outcome variable are restricted to white respondents. The authors thus control for race by restricting their analysis to one racial subsample, but do not examine its net effects or compare the results for whites with the results for blacks.

Herrnstein and Murray then repeat this analysis for different subsamples to determine the moderating effects of education, marital status, and sex on being in poverty. To examine the effect of education, they compare the results of the same regression for a sample of high school graduates and a sample of college graduates. Their main finding is that hardly any college graduates were in poverty, while among high school graduates, test scores were again more important than socioeconomic background in determining whether a respondent was in poverty. Herrnstein and Murray then replicate the same analysis for a sample of married mothers and a sample of mothers who were separated, divorced, or never married. They again report that the test score variable handily beats parental socioeconomic status in explaining poverty.

While Herrnstein and Murray repeatedly claim that adding education, marital status, and gender makes the analysis sufficiently complex to satisfy the more critical reader, it is the "simple picture" (Herrnstein and Murray, 1994:141) that best captures their view of the situation. This simple picture holds that, at least for whites, intelligence is by far a stronger predictor of poverty than parental socioeconomic status, and analyses of the causes of poverty need to be rectified to reflect the crucial role of intelligence.

While Herrnstein and Murray prefer to look at the "simple picture," the authors of *Inequality by Design* favor a much more complex and exhaustive model of the causes poverty. Using the same sample of NLSY respondents, Fischer et al. attempt to refute Herrnstein and Murray's findings by adding a variety of other variables to the analysis, thereby hoping to show that the effect of test scores on poverty is in fact not nearly as large as Herrnstein and Murray claim. After reproducing the results of Herrnstein and Murray and correcting their technical mistakes, Fischer et al. gradually add more measures of respondents' social background, education, and living conditions into the mix of independent variables. While Herrnstein and Murray's simple model contains only 3 variables, the fully specified model of Fischer et al. includes some 29 variables.[2] Once all these variables are included, the importance of the test score variable appears in a different light. In the analyses of Fischer et al., social background—measured as the attributes of a respondent's family and community—was just as important as test scores in predicting poverty. They found that respondents' formal schooling and gender were also important predictors. While Herrnstein and Murray had conducted separate analyses for married and unmarried mothers, Fischer

---

2. This number includes 24 substantive variables and 5 control variables for missing data values that were replaced with the respective variable's mean value.

et al. include these conditions as variables in their model. They conclude that when it comes to explaining variation in poverty, the test score variable is "relatively far down on the list of risk factors for poverty"(1996:92). This conclusion is reinforced when using explained variation as a measure of model fit. To assess the explanatory power of Herrnstein and Murray's test score variable, Fischer et al. compare their fully specified model with the same model omitting AFQT scores. Excluding test scores reduces the pseudo R^2 to .315 from .322, a difference of less than one percentage point. In short, they find that very little of the variation in poverty is uniquely explained by test scores.

Conclusion

For the reasons we have shown, the study of the causes of poverty is an appropriate empirical site for our demonstration of the usefulness of intersectional methods. In studying poverty, a number of academic disciplines converge, and the available data have been examined from a variety of different angles. In focusing on the debate over the effects of test scores on the likelihood of being in poverty, we have argued that the debate tends to suffer from an undue concern for the exact contribution of predictor variables, engaged in a competition to explain variation. We focused on two approaches to studying poverty: the "simple picture" approach of *The Bell Curve*, which includes only a bare minimum of predictor variables, and the "everything but the kitchen sink" approach of *Inequality by Design*, which includes a large variety of predictor variables. While the test score variable wins the race against socioeconomic background in *The Bell Curve*, the same variable withers when confronted with the variables championed by the authors of *Inequality by Design*.

In chapter 3, we present a reanalysis of the logistic regressions published by Herrnstein and Murray and Fischer et al. We then compare the results of both efforts with respect to how well this methodology performs in actually predicting who is in poverty and who is not. Finally, we report the results from alternate regression models containing only a modest number of explanatory variables, thus providing a baseline for our intersectional analysis.

THREE

Explaining Poverty: The Key Causal Conditions

In this chapter we present a conventional quantitative analysis of the *Bell Curve* data, focusing on the key causal conditions in the debate on race, class, test scores, and poverty. Like Herrnstein and Murray and Fischer et al., we use logistic regression techniques in this chapter to analyze the NLSY data. However, we avoid their extremes, the radically underspecified analysis of Herrnstein and Murray and the bloated overspecified analysis of Fischer et al. Instead, we present a middle path between these two, focusing on only the most important variables. Our analysis offers not only a middle path, but also a baseline for comparison with the fuzzy-set analyses we present in subsequent chapters, as our fuzzy-set analyses are based on the variables that we use in this chapter.[1]

Before presenting our logistic regression analysis of the key causal conditions, we first reproduce and evaluate the findings reported by Fischer et al. Our goal in the reanalysis of Fischer et al.'s findings is to assess their model, first with respect to its accuracy and then with respect to its explanatory power. We demonstrate that despite its dramatic reduction of the effect of test scores on the odds of avoiding poverty, their analysis is less effective when assessed through the lens of predicted outcomes—the percentage of cases correctly assigned to each of the two possible outcomes, *in-poverty* and *not-in-poverty*.

After evaluating Fischer et al.'s analysis, we describe the operationalization and measurement of what we consider to be the most important causal conditions in the *Bell Curve* debate. Of course, our selection of causal conditions is limited by the data we use—the National Longitudinal Survey

---

1. In chapter 4 we document how we transform these variables into fuzzy sets, using techniques developed by Ragin (2008) for calibrating degree of set membership.

of Youth—but this limitation is shared by the many researchers who have participated in this debate. Nevertheless, it is useful to hold the data set "constant" in order to demonstrate the value added of the set-analytic approach. Our main independent variables are race, gender, parental income, parental education, respondent's education, respondent's test scores, and respondent's household composition (marital status and dependents). The dependent variable in all the analyses reported in this chapter is poverty status, a dichotomous outcome variable indicating whether the respondent's household income is above or below the poverty level.

The choice of causal conditions is a nontrivial one, especially for our fuzzy-set analyses. In a conventional net effects analysis, such as logistic regression, bad choices sometimes fall by the wayside, for they may fail to register significant effects on the dependent variable. Of course, this convenient resolution does not always occur, and specification errors may skew all the estimates in a given model and lead to erroneous conclusions. In set-theoretic analyses, poor choices can have a greater impact, because these analyses examine all possible combinations of causal conditions; that is, these analyses are fully "intersectional." It is more difficult to "drop" a causal condition from a set-theoretic analysis because the condition must be shown to be inconsequential in many different contexts. For these reasons, it is wise to keep the list of causal conditions relatively short and to focus on causal conditions of greatest interest and known importance. Of course, the problem of omitted variables has a detrimental impact on both conventional net effects analysis and intersectional analysis. Fortunately, there is considerable consensus among scholars using survey data regarding which variables matter most when it comes to assessing the causal conditions linked to poverty, and our analyses include all key explanatory variables employed by both Herrnstein and Murray and Fischer et al.

In the third and final major section of this chapter, we present the results of our logistic regression analyses. We compute four analyses based on a division of the NLSY sample into four subsamples: black females, black males, white females, and white males. We follow this same strategy in the fuzzy-set analyses presented in subsequent chapters, with separate analyses presented for each subsample.

Reproducing Fischer et al.'s Findings

To better evaluate the findings of both *The Bell Curve* and *Inequality by Design*, we re-created both analyses, aiming to match their results as closely as possible. We used data generously provided by Richard Arum, one of the coauthors of *Inequality by Design*, and also the original NLSY data set. As noted previously, it is a simple matter to reproduce the primitive *Bell Curve* analysis. However, while we were able to closely match the results reported by Fischer et al., we encountered difficulties in confirming some of their results, in regard to three variables: the *Married Man* (1990) interaction term, the *School Composition* measure, and the *Unemployment Rate* (1990) variable. In an appendix to this chapter, we detail how we addressed these three issues.

Tables 3.1a and 3.1b give our closest reproduction of tables A2.3 (whites only) and A2.4 (blacks only) reported in *Inequality by Design*. These tables summarize the results of the logistic regression analyses that underlie most of the arguments presented in chapter 4 of their book.[2] For the most part, our results closely match those presented by Fischer et al. Effect sizes, directions, and significance levels all exhibit the same patterns. Some minor differences may be explained by a slightly different number of cases, but overall we were able to almost perfectly reproduce the tables reported in *Inequality by Design*.[3]

Tables 3.2a and 3.2b give our own versions of the same models, but this time with the corrected interaction variable for married men and the disaggregated composite of the adolescent school environment (as discussed in the appendix to this chapter). When compared to tables A2.3 and A2.4 of *Inequality by Design*, it is clear that, except for the corrected variables, the overall pattern remains very similar. In the following discussion, we focus on this second set of equations, the corrected set.

After replicating the results of *The Bell Curve* and *Inequality by Design*, the next step is to evaluate their performance. There are several ways to estimate how well a logistic regression model fits the data. One of the simplest yet most informative criteria for evaluating the quality of a model is to compare the model's predicted outcomes with the outcomes actually observed in order to assess how many respondents the statistical model classifies correctly.

---

2. Fischer et al. also reproduce *The Bell Curve* model, with several important corrections. This model, which includes only test scores, socioeconomic status, and age as predictors, represents an improvement over the model reported in *The Bell Curve*. Because of its simplicity, this model is easy to reproduce, and we do not report our own reproduction of the results reported in *The Bell* Curve.

3. The difference in the number of cases in our model versus that of Fischer et al. is 3,034 versus 3,031 for the sample of white respondents and 1,725 versus 1,726 for the sample of black respondents.

Table 3.1a Reproduction of table A2.3 of Fischer et al. 1996. Logistic regression of likelihood of a person being in poverty in 1990 (whites only).

	(A1)	(A2)	(A3)	(A4)	(A5)	(A6)	(A7)	(A8)	(A9)
Intercept	-2.8536**	-2.8816**	-2.7953**	-3.4740**	-1.1540	-1.6239	-.5757	1.5101	3.2550**
	(.0885)	(.0898)	(.2461)	(.3052)	(.9097)	(.9240)	(.9596)	(1.1302)	(1.0286)
ZZAFQT	-.8434**	-.7028**	-.6839**	-.6566**	-.4439**	-.4425**	-.4424**	-.3989**	-.3886**
	(.0716)	(.0802)	(.0823)	(.0840)	(.0977)	(.0977)	(.1001)	(.1073)	(.1343)
SES		-.2978**							
		(.0802)							
Age		-.0478	-.0834	-.0242	-.0675	-.0660	-.0131	.0095	.0272
		(.0738)	(.0842)	(.0846)	(.1084)	(.1086)	(.1095)	(.1188)	(.1179)
Family Income			-.4443**	-.4293**	-.4189**	-.4071**	-.4098**	-.3717**	-.3886**
			(.1218)	(.1231)	(.1245)	(.1241)	(.1249)	(.1342)	(.1343)
Parents' SEI			-.0734	-.0619	-.0439	-.0318	-.0223	-.0429	-.0658
			(.0857)	(.0877)	(.0893)	(.0895)	(.0903)	(.1005)	(.0990)
Mother's education			.0048	-.0323	.0065	.0071	.0302	.0643	.0359
			(.0895)	(.0910)	(.0934)	(.0937)	(.0942)	(.1022)	(.1016)
Father's education			-.0334	-.0355	.0139	.0183	.0153	-.0050	-.0389
			(.0986)	(.1002)	(.1036)	(.1041)	(.1060)	(.1162)	(.1151)
Siblings (1979)			.1839**	.1733**	.1440*	.1500*	.1475*	.0467	.0407
			(.0650)	(.0672)	(.0684)	(.0688)	(.0695)	(.0765)	(.0761)
Farm background			-.2593	-.3364	-.3417	-.3758	-.2517	-.2863	-.3471
			(.3120)	(.3171)	(.3172)	(.3219)	(.3228)	(.3605)	(.3563)
Two-parent family			-.2331	-.1184	-.1392	-.1324	-.1175	-.0691	-.0320
			(.2375)	(.2446)	(.2455)	(.2463)	(.2488)	(.2756)	(.2729)
Missing fam. income			.0236	.0811	.0846	.0592	.0183	.0484	.0662
			(.2855)	(.2875)	(.2900)	(.2906)	(.2940)	(.3161)	(.3126)

	(1)	(2)	(3)	(4)	(5)	(6)	(7)
Independent (Miss. Inc.)	.4365 (.3395)	.2163 (.3415)	.1258 (.3422)	.1030 (.3428)	-.0710 (.3464)	-.1877 (.3792)	-.2657 (.3750)
Missing parents' SEI	-.1740 (.3237)	-.2032 (.3329)	-.1868 (.3349)	-.2132 (.3355)	-.2323 (.3398)	-.1109 (.3730)	.0124 (.3698)
Missing mother's ed.	-.0806 (.3556)	.0052 (.3546)	-.0660 (.3545)	-.0607 (.3557)	-.0150 (.3603)	.0637 (.4097)	.1822 (.4002)
Missing father's ed.	.3615 (.2659)	.4171 (.2663)	.3695 (.2658)	.3955 (.2677)	.3568 (.2706)	.2541 (.3063)	.2485 (.3035)
School composition		-.2503** (.0670)	-.2483** (.0674)	-.2425** (.0677)	-.2468** (.0686)	-.2740** (.0749)	-.2994** (.0744)
Missing school report		.4763** (.1652)	.4979** (.1674)	.5013** (.1684)	.4337* (.1703)	.2038 (.1905)	.2127 (.1897)
West region		.9174** (.2249)	.8894** (.2283)	.8139** (.2378)	.8499** (.2397)	.5615* (.2609)	.5579* (.2591)
Northeast region		.0685 (.2759)	.1246 (.2785)	.1216 (.2852)	.1381 (.2875)	-.0160 (.3099)	-.0372 (.3072)
Central region		.6202** (.2018)	.6240** (.2040)	.5230* (.2139)	.5437* (.2164)	.3232 (.2334)	.3284 (.2326)
Years of ed. pre–AFQT			-.1619* (.0734)	-.1635* (.0735)	-.2247** (.0758)	-.2564** (.0827)	-.3849** (.0758)
H.S. academic track			-.4756 (.2564)	-.4574 (.2573)	-.4642 (.2580)	-.2022 (.2736)	-.3302 (.2681)
Years of ed. post–AFQT			-.2222** (.0676)	-.2310** (.0682)	-.2286** (.0681)	-.1922** (.0708)	-.2555** (.0685)
Unemployment rate (1990)				.0839* (.0419)	.0813 (.0423)	.0690 (.0467)	.0711 (.0463)
Central city (1990)				.5069 (.2681)	.5625* (.2699)	.4865 (.2855)	.4240 (.2842)

(continued)

Table 3.1a (*continued*)

	(A1)	(A2)	(A3)	(A4)	(A5)	(A6)	(A7)	(A8)	(A9)
Rural (1990)						.0862	.1058	.0972	.0939
						(.1920)	(.1935)	(.2124)	(.2103)
Male							-.8369**	-.9813**	-1.0098**
							(.1646)	(.2252)	(.2224)
Children (1990)								.7257**	.7187**
								(.0887)	(.0876)
Married (1990)								-3.0791**	-3.1207**
								(.2574)	(.2574)
Married man (1990)								-.5243**	-.5545**
								(.1801)	(.1789)
Pseudo R^2	0.0948	0.1037	0.1209	0.1461	0.1607	0.1660	0.1833	0.3239	0.3150

Table 3.1b Reproduction of table A2.4 of Fischer et al. 1996. Logistic regression of likelihood of a person being in poverty in 1990 (African Americans only).

	(B1)	(B2)	(B3)	(B4)	(B5)	(B6)	(B7)	(B8)	(B9)
Intercept	-1.1171**	-1.1513**	-1.2421**	-1.7510**	2.3282**	1.5516**	2.7068**	2.2394*	3.3361**
	(.0601)	(.0617)	(.1380)	(.1607)	(.6715)	(.7074)	(.7462)	(.9118)	(.8664)
ZZAFQT	-.8031**	-.6869**	-.6858**	-.6706**	-.3736**	-.3707**	-.3919**	-.3679**	-.2545*
	(.0674)	(.0707)	(.0725)	(.0745)	(.0849)	(.0854)	(.0884)	(.0942)	(.1058)
SES		-.3488**							
		(.0630)							
Age		-.0462	-.0555	-.0400	-.0110	.0002	.0180	-.0081	-.0086
		(.0582)	(.0638)	(.0651)	(.0820)	(.0821)	(.0842)	(.0896)	(.0891)
Family income			-.2812**	-.3396**	-.3266**	-.3091**	-.2686**	-.2411*	-.2545*
			(.0948)	(.0990)	(.1005)	(.1016)	(.1003)	(.1046)	(.1058)
Parents' SEI			-.2085**	-.2240**	-.2333**	-.2354**	-.2620**	-.2045*	-.2302**
			(.0770)	(.0778)	(.0803)	(.0808)	(.0826)	(.0871)	(.0866)
Mother's education			-.1234	-.1601*	-.0860	-.0867	-.0451	-.0197	-.0399
			(.0727)	(.0742)	(.0764)	(.0769)	(.0791)	(.0855)	(.0844)
Father's education			.0253	.0307	.0747	.0827	.0864	.0838	.0754
			(.0836)	(.0852)	(.0878)	(.0883)	(.0900)	(.0971)	(.0963)
Siblings (1979)			-.0528	-.0340	-.0605	-.0659	-.0704*	-.0470	-.0233
			(.0629)	(.0642)	(.0658)	(.0662)	(.0681)	(.0725)	(.0715)
Farm background			-.2033	.0083	-.1179	-.2210	-.1866	-.2731	-.2332
			(.3549)	(.3570)	(.3639)	(.3689)	(.3844)	(.4303)	(.4239)
Two-parent family			-.1311	-.0755	-.0457	-.0346	-.0234	.0006	.0184
			(.1435)	(.1473)	(.1500)	(.1513)	(.1542)	(.1637)	(.1627)
Missing fam. income			-.2070	-.2039	-.1971	-.2448	-.2144	-.2729	-.1924
			(.2269)	(.2305)	(.2348)	(.2372)	(.2412)	(.2595)	(.2596)

(continued)

Table 3.1b (continued)

	(B1)	(B2)	(B3)	(B4)	(B5)	(B6)	(B7)	(B8)	(B9)
Independent (Miss. Inc.)			.7454* (.2988)	.7028* (.3044)	.6018 (.3128)	.6367* (.3155)	.4117 (.3241)	.3829 (.3482)	.2807 (.3445)
Missing parents' SEI			.3183 (.1645)	.1514 (.1705)	.1488 (.1753)	.1158 (.1765)	.1365 (.1801)	.1076 (.1907)	.1420 (.1901)
Missing mother's Ed.			.0692 (.2141)	.0931 (.2166)	-.0562 (.2219)	-.0386 (.2230)	-.0083 (.2305)	.0519 (.2438)	.0845 (.2439)
Missing father's Ed.			.2022 (.1420)	.1931 (.1445)	.1604 (.1470)	.1832 (.1481)	.1919 (.1528)	.1238 (.1618)	.1422 (.1605)
School composition				-.2609** (.0695)	-.2443** (.0703)	-.2643** (.0724)	-.2420** (.0737)	-.2572** (.0790)	-.2781** (.0784)
Missing school report				.5905** (.1543)	.5251** (.1575)	.5813** (.1612)	.5246** (.1643)	.5234** (.1754)	.5958** (.1732)
West region				.6637* (.2612)	.6908** (.2640)	.6407* (.2717)	.6643* (.2793)	.5959* (.2915)	.6347* (.2900)
Northeast region				.4575* (.1879)	.3509 (.1939)	.2453 (.2041)	.3301 (.2064)	.2002 (.2147)	.1086 (.2131)
Central region				.8194** (.1557)	.8056** (.1580)	.7439** (.1633)	.7879** (.1675)	.5607** (.1799)	.5034** (.1774)
Years of ed. pre-AFQT					-.3210** (.0562)	-.3141** (.0567)	-.3797** (.0592)	-.3396** (.0630)	-.4257** (.0589)
H.S. academic track					-.4250** (.1640)	-.4280** (.1650)	-.3966* (.1673)	-.3518* (.1769)	-.4410* (.1742)
Years of ed. post-AFQT					-.247** (.0556)	-.2406** (.0559)	-.2581** (.0572)	-.2076** (.0607)	-.2612** (.0586)

Unemployment rate (1990)						.1205** (.0401)	.1218** (.0410)	.1318** (.0441)	.1310** (.0437)
Central city (1990)						.1590 (.1534)	.1611 (.1569)	.0412 (.1663)	.0664 (.1650)
Rural (1990)						.2014 (.1672)	.1977 (.1709)	.2698 (.1830)	.2883 (.1821)
Male							-.9860** (.1333)	-.6470** (.1703)	-.6464** (.1692)
Children (1990)								.4225** (.0607)	.4166** (.0604)
Married (1990)								-2.0231** (.2263)	-2.0638** (.2254)
Married man (1990)								-.0797 (.1807)	-.0957 (.1803)
Pseudo R^2	0.0859	0.1021	0.1175	0.1469	0.1768	0.1831	0.2121	0.2907	0.2829

Table 3.2a Improved version of table A2.3 of Fischer et al. 1996. Logistic regression of likelihood of a person being in poverty in 1990 (whites only).

	(A1)	(A2)	(A3)	(A4)	(A5)	(A6)	(A7)	(A8)	(A9)
Intercept	-2.8535**	-2.8816**	-2.7953**	-3.3359**	-1.0545	-1.5690	-.5260	.5255	2.2968
	(.0885)	(.0898)	(.2461)	(.3099)	(.9167)	(.9324)	(.9679)	(1.0577)	(.9546)
ZZAFQT	-.8434**	-.7028**	-.6839**	-.6631**	-.4511**	-.4489**	-.4494**	-.4104**	
	(.0716)	(.0806)	(.0823)	(.0842)	(.0979)	(.0979)	(.1004)	(.1078)	
SES		-.2973							
		(.0802)							
Age		-.0478	-.0834	-.0210	-.0673	-.0644	-.0130	.0097	.0273
		(.0738)	(.0842)	(.0849)	(.1083)	(.1086)	(.1096)	(.1189)	(.1179)
Family income			-.4443**	-.4419**	-.4328*	-.4199**	-.4194**	-.3781**	-.3957**
			(.1218)	(.1234)	(.1248)	(.1243)	(.1252)	(.1343)	(.1346)
Parents' SEI			-.0734	-.0736	-.0560	-.0444	-.0336	-.0475	-.0692
			(.0857)	(.0882)	(.0898)	(.0900)	(.0908)	(.1008)	(.0993)
Mother's education			.0048	-.0345	.0048	.0058	.0297	.0651	.0342
			(.0895)	(.0908)	(.0932)	(.0935)	(.0908)	(.1019)	(.1013)
Father's education			-.0334	-.0418	.0071	.0111	.0082	-.0134	-.0476
			(.0986)	(.1001)	(.1035)	(.1038)	(.1057)	(.1159)	(.1147)
Siblings (1979)			.1839**	.1685**	.1385*	.1429*	.1410*	.0399	.0351
			(.0650)	(.0675)	(.0687)	(.0691)	(.0699)	(.0768)	(.0765)
Farm background			-.2593	-.2899	-.2868	-.3402	-.2153	-.2634	-.3220
			(.3120)	(.3185)	(.3184)	(.3219)	(.3229)	(.3604)	(.3563)
Two-parent family			-.2331	-.0919	-.1163	-.1073	-.0969	-.0544	-.0171
			(.2375)	(.2451)	(.2457)	(.2466)	(.2491)	(.2759)	(.2731)
Missing fam. Income			.0236	.0723	.0799	.0416	-.0035	.0369	.0601
			(.2855)	(.2885)	(.2911)	(.2925)	(.2961)	(.3167)	(.3132)

	(1)	(2)	(3)	(4)	(5)	(6)	(7)
Independent (Miss. Inc.)	.4365 (.3395)	.2049 (.3422)	.1107 (.3431)	.0952 (.3442)	-.0700 (.3481)	-.2059 (.3800)	-.2872 (.3757)
Missing parents' SEI	-.1740 (.3237)	-.1746 (.3314)	-.1546 (.3335)	-.1722 (.3336)	-.1909 (.3375)	-.0750 (.3714)	.0510 (.3681)
Missing mother's ed.	-.0806 (.3556)	.0048 (.3571)	-.0741 (.3570)	-.0606 (.3581)	-.0149 (.3622)	.0780 (.4106)	.1868 (.4027)
Missing father's ed.	.3615 (.2659)	.4142 (.2675)	.3616 (.2671)	.3906 (.2692)	.3576 (.2722)	.2448 (.3079)	.2415 (.3047)
Fewer dropout students		-.1963** (.0729)	-.1919** (.0743)	-.2016** (.0740)	-.2000** (.0754)	-.2161** (.0831)	-.2251** (.0824)
Fewer disad. students		-.0284 (.1257)	-.0207 (.1262)	.0232 (.1269)	.0079 (.1280)	-.0431 (.1375)	-.0695 (.1363)
Fewer nonwhite students		-.3119* (.1384)	-.3310* (.1395)	-.3490* (.1434)	-.3420* (.1441)	-.3221* (.1552)	-.3547* (.1554)
Missing dropout stud.		-.0428 (.3927)	.0651 (.3907)	.0239 (.3922)	-.0358 (.3941)	-.0963 (.4489)	.0363 (.4316)
Missing disad. stud.		.1589 (.2368)	.1758 (.2376)	.2093 (.2396)	.2033 (.2421)	.1576 (.2619)	.1133 (.2592)
Missing nonwhite stud.		.3189 (.3939)	.2138 (.3941)	.2274 (.3941)	.2183 (.3940)	.0902 (.4415)	-.0196 (.4286)
West region		.8927** (.2258)	.8566** (.2291)	.7905** (.2380)	.8274** (.2401)	.5445* (.2608)	.5416* (.2593)
Northeast region		.0397 (.2760)	.0947 (.2785)	.1081 (.2860)	.1266 (.2881)	-.0345 (.3104)	-.0521 (.3078)
Central region		.5799** (.2033)	.5782** (.2054)	.4813* (.2161)	.5057* (.2183)	.2806 (.2353)	.2907 (.2349)
Years of ed. pre-AFQT			-.1575* (.0736)	-.1575* (.0737)	-.2182** (.0761)	-.2489** (.0829)	-.3817** (.0760)
H.S. academic track			-.4899 (.2568)	-.4795 (.2578)	-.4695 (.2584)	-.2177 (.2737)	-.3502 (.2683)

(continued)

Table 3.2a *(continued)*

	(A1)	(A2)	(A3)	(A4)	(A5)	(A6)	(A7)	(A8)	(A9)
Years of ed. post-AFQT					-.2235**	-.2326**	-.2295**	-.1910**	-.2550**
					(.0676)	(.0684)	(.0684)	(.0711)	(.0689)
Unemployment rate						.0833*	.0809	.0701	.0710
(1990)						(.0423)	(.0426)	(.0472)	(.0467)
Central city						.5186	.5749*	.4892	.4270
(1990)						(.2696)	(.2714)	(.2868)	(.2853)
Rural						.1534	.1706	.1410	.1406
(1990)						(.1970)	(.1988)	(.2183)	(.2159)
Male							-.8219**	-.9718**	-.9973**
							(.1649)	(.2254)	(.2226)
Children								.7213**	.7141**
(1990)								(.0887)	(.0875)
Married								-3.0629**	-3.1043**
(1990)								(.2569)	(.2570)
Married man								1.0432**	1.1044**
(1990)								(.3605)	(.3576)
Pseudo R^2	0.0948	0.1037	0.1209	0.1475	0.1623	0.1682	0.1849	0.3238	0.3145

Table 3.2b Improved version of table A2.4 of Fischer et al. 1996. Logistic regression of likelihood of a person being in poverty in 1990 (African Americans only).

	(B1)	(B2)	(B3)	(B4)	(B5)	(B6)	(B7)	(B8)	(B9)
Intercept	-1.1171**	-1.1513**	-1.2421**	-1.8619**	2.2524**	1.4507*	2.6735**	2.0534**	3.0998**
	(.0601)	(.0617)	(.1380)	(.1788)	(.6820)	(.7195)	(.7604)	(.8249)	(.7762)
ZZAFQT	-.8031**	-.6869**	-.6858**	-.6705**	-.3731**	-.3695**	-.3905**	-.3638**	
	(.0674)	(.0707)	(.0725)	(.0746)	(.0850)	(.0856)	(.0884)	(.0945)	
SES		-.3488							
		(.0630)							
Age		-.0462	-.0555	-.0364	-.0111	.0003	.0186	-.0088	-.0094
		(.0582)	(.0638)	(.0658)	(.0821)	(.0822)	(.0844)	(.0900)	(.0894)
Family income			-.2812**	-.3435**	-.3309**	-.3152**	-.2719**	-.2499*	-.2629*
			(.0948)	(.0994)	(.1009)	(.1019)	(.1005)	(.1050)	(.1062)
Parents' SEI			-.2085**	-.2221**	-.2307**	-.2330**	-.2604**	-.2007*	-.2269**
			(.0770)	(.0780)	(.0805)	(.0810)	(.0828)	(.0873)	(.0868)
Mother's education			-.1234	-.1613*	-.0851	-.0851	-.0437	-.0173	-.0368
			(.0727)	(.0744)	(.0765)	(.0770)	(.0794)	(.0857)	(.0847)
Father's education			.0253	.0369	.0811	.0881	.0924	.0917	.0839
			(.0836)	(.0853)	(.0879)	(.0884)	(.0901)	(.0971)	(.0963)
Siblings (1979)			-.0528	-.0354	-.0615	-.0662	-.0732	-.0464	-.0228
			(.0629)	(.0645)	(.0661)	(.0665)	(.0684)	(.0729)	(.0719)
Farm background			-.2033	-.0053	-.1177	-.2188	-.1889	-.2558	-.2127
			(.3549)	(.3592)	(.3658)	(.3701)	(.3858)	(.4323)	(.4262)
Two-parent family			-.1311	-.0843	-.0558	-.0431	-.0376	-.0143	.0022
			(.1435)	(.1477)	(.1503)	(.1516)	(.1546)	(.1643)	(.1633)
Missing fam. income			-.2070	-.2039	-.2022	-.2530	-.2189	-.2863	-.2079
			(.2269)	(.2309)	(.2351)	(.2376)	(.2419)	(.2599)	(.2600)

(continued)

Table 3.2b (*continued*)

	(B1)	(B2)	(B3)	(B4)	(B5)	(B6)	(B7)	(B8)	(B9)
Independent (Miss. Inc.)			.7454* (.2988)	.7011* (.3053)	.6119 (.3137)	.6491* (.3166)	.4181 (.3254)	.3977 (.3493)	.2968 (.3457)
Missing parents' SEI			.3183 (.1645)	.1473 (.1710)	.1471 (.1758)	.1137 (.1770)	.1325 (.1807)	.1115 (.1917)	.1477 (.1911)
Missing mother's ed.			.0692 (.2141)	.0921 (.2167)	-.0609 (.2219)	-.0429 (.2229)	-.0123 (.2305)	.0490 (.2434)	.0817 (.2434)
Missing father's ed.			.2022 (.1420)	.1862 (.1448)	.1503 (.1472)	.1730 (.1483)	.1843 (.1530)	.1115 (.1623)	.1275 (.1610)
Fewer dropout students				-.1257 (.0766)	-.0602 (.0799)	-.0761 (.0814)	-.0572 (.0820)	-.0575 (.0863)	-.0567 (.0862)
Fewer disad. students				-.1519 (.0808)	-.1543 (.0826)	-.1513 (.0837)	-.1648 (.0858)	-.1482 (.0913)	-.1620 (.0913)
Fewer nonwhite students				-.1096 (.0940)	-.1405 (.0956)	-.1629 (.0997)	-.1373 (.1012)	-.1832 (.1075)	-.1999 (.1070)
Missing dropout stud.				-.0028 (.3236)	-.1006 (.3272)	-.0725 (.3311)	-.1855 (.3408)	-.3428 (.3604)	-.3495 (.3577)
Missing disad. stud.				.1306 (.2117)	.1659 (.2155)	.1914 (.2196)	.1221 (.2252)	.1929 (.2420)	.2221 (.2415)
Missing nonwhite stud.				.4012 (.3523)	.4268 (.3560)	.4367 (.3613)	.5534 (.3693)	.6538 (.3860)	.7071 (.3825)
West region				.6579* (.2626)	.7042** (.2658)	.6560* (.2738)	.6821* (.2816)	.6189* (.2935)	.6616* (.2920)
Northeast region				.4669* (.1884)	.3560 (.1945)	.2505 (.2043)	.3368 (.2065)	.2105 (.2152)	.1208 (.2137)
Central region				.8355** (.1577)	.8133** (.1600)	.7524** (.1645)	.7981** (.1689)	.5757** (.1816)	.5206** (.1792)

	(1)	(2)	(3)	(4)	(5)	(6)	(7)	(8)	(9)
Years of ed. pre-AFQT					-.3260** (.0572)	-.3184** (.0575)	-.3861** (.0602)	-.3490** (.0641)	-.4351** (.0600)
H.S. academic track					-.4330** (.1646)	-.4362** (.1655)	-.4025* (.1679)	-.3631* (.1776)	-.4513** (.1749)
Years of ed. post-AFQT					-.2460** (.0557)	-.2400** (.0560)	-.2566** (.0573)	-.2092** (.0609)	-.2617** (.0588)
Unemployment rate (1990)						.1200** (.0406)	.1177** (.0414)	.1282** (.0444)	.1273** (.0441)
Central city (1990)						.1553 (.1559)	.1689 (.1598)	.0372 (.1698)	.0613 (.1684)
Rural (1990)						.2053 (.1706)	.2118 (.1745)	.2774 (.1870)	.2974 (.1861)
Male							-.9978** (.1338)	-.6644** (.1712)	-.6653** (.1701)
Children (1990)								.4252** (.0609)	.4200** (.0607)
Married (1990)								-2.0396** (.2272)	-2.0829** (.2264)
Married man (1990)								.1896 (.3629)	.2241 (.3621)
Pseudo R^2	0.0859	0.1021	0.1175	0.1469	0.1771	0.1833	0.2129	0.2917	0.2841

Table 3.3 Cases predicted correctly and incorrectly, whites and blacks.

Observed Cases	Cases not in poverty specified correctly	Percentage of cases not in poverty specified correctly[1]	Cases in poverty specified correctly	Percentage of cases in poverty specified correctly[2]	Total cases specified correctly	Overall percentage of cases specified correctly
Not In Poverty: 2,813 In Poverty: 221	whites only ($n = 3,034$)					
Model A1	2813	100.00	0	0.00	2813	92.72
Model A2 (*Bell Curve* Model)	2811	99.93	0	0.00	2811	92.65
Model A3	2812	99.96	3	1.36	2815	92.78
Model A4	2811	99.93	12	5.43	2823	93.05
Model A5	2811	99.93	9	4.07	2820	92.95
Model A6	2809	99.86	12	5.43	2821	92.98
Model A7	2801	99.57	17	7.69	2818	92.88
Model A8 (IBD Model)	2781	98.86	57	25.79	2838	93.54
Model A9	2783	98.93	56	25.34	2839	93.57
Not In Poverty: 1,270 In Poverty: 455	blacks only ($n = 1,725$)					
Model A1	1217	95.83	57	12.53	1274	73.86
Model A2 (*Bell Curve* Model)	1217	95.83	77	16.92	1294	75.01
Model A3	1204	94.80	100	21.98	1304	75.59
Model A4	1190	93.70	140	30.77	1330	77.10
Model A5	1182	93.07	163	35.82	1345	77.97
Model A6	1177	92.68	167	36.70	1344	77.91
Model A7	1175	92.52	194	42.64	1369	79.36
Model A8 (IBD Model)	1179	92.83	236	51.87	1415	82.03
Model A9	1179	92.83	233	51.21	1412	81.86

[1] Number of cases not in poverty predicted / number of cases not in poverty observed.
[2] Number of cases in poverty predicted / number of cases in poverty observed.

Table 3.3 reports the performance of the different models using this criterion, comparing the *Bell Curve* model of Herrnstein and Murray with our improved versions of Fischer et al.'s models.

Regarding the white sample, the most striking finding that emerges is the lack of explanatory power of Herrnstein and Murray's model. Specifically, the basic *Bell Curve* model does not predict correctly a single respondent who experienced poverty. In fact, of the first seven equations, not a single model specifies more than about 8% of those in poverty correctly. The fully specified model A8, which is Fischer et al.'s favored model, predicts substantially more cases correctly, but even this model correctly predicts only about a quarter of those in poverty.

For all models, the overall percentage of cases predicted correctly is relatively high, between 92.7% and 93.6%. However, this success rate is not nearly as impressive as it may seem at first glance. Given the fact that the vast majority of respondents did not experience poverty, merely guessing that *all* respondents are out of poverty would prove correct 92.7% of the time (i.e., the raw percentage of respondents not in poverty). The first two models thus offer no improvement over this baseline, as they fail to correctly predict even a single case actually in poverty.[4] However, even the fully specified model A8 reduces the classification errors by only about 12% (from 7.28% predicted incorrectly to 6.46%).

For the sample of black respondents, the model performs somewhat better. Still, the basic *Bell Curve* model correctly classifies only about 17% of those actually in poverty, while the fully specified model A8 manages to classify about 52% of those in poverty correctly. But even for these models, the reduction of errors of classification is modest. For blacks, merely guessing that no one was in poverty would have proved correct 73.6% of the time, which is only slightly lower than the 75.01% correctly predicted by Herrnstein and Murray's model. The fully specified model A8 performs somewhat better, but even this model reduces classification errors by only about a quarter (from 26.14% incorrect to 17.97% incorrect).

Another way to evaluate the fit of a logistic regression model is to calculate the pseudo R^2 value as a measure of the proportion of variation accounted for by the independent variables. If we use this criterion, it appears that the basic *Bell Curve* model explains only about 10% of the variance in poverty, for both blacks and whites. In other words, if we consider only test scores, age, and socioeconomic status, then this model fails to account for 90% of the variation in poverty outcomes. Given this rather low explanatory power, the claim by Herrnstein and Murray that their analyses make a powerful case for sweeping policy changes (1994:142) seems ludicrous. As for model A8, the one favored by the authors of *Inequality by Design*, this model explains about a third of the variation in white poverty, and slightly less in

---

4. Technically, the *Bell Curve* model performs slighly worse than a mere guess, but this is beside the point.

black poverty. Clearly, the model of Fischer et al. is substantially better, but even with this model about two-thirds of the variation in poverty outcomes remains unexplained.

It thus seems that none of the logistic regression models does a particularly effective job of classifying cases. However, there are at least two further insights to be gained from the analyses just presented. First, using conventional statistical methods, there appear to be significant differences in the ability to predict poverty for blacks and whites. In fact, if we examine how many cases are predicted correctly, it appears to be much easier to predict poverty for blacks than for whites. This insight has important consequences for studying the causes of poverty, because it suggests that the paths that lead blacks into or out of poverty are much more limited in their diversity, while the paths for whites are much more diverse and thus more difficult to model using conventional methods.

Second, the large increase in explanatory power between models A7 and A8 in the sample of white respondents offers some insights into the importance of the newly included variables. In model A8, three variables were added: *children* (1990), *married* (1990), and *married-man* (1990). For whites, these three variables alone increase the number of cases in poverty specified correctly from about 8% to about 26%. For black respondents, the increase is less dramatic (from 43% to about 52% of cases specified correctly), but again the largest increase in the percentage of cases predicted correctly is achieved when moving from model A7 to model A8.

Using the pseudo R^2 as a fit measure, we see a similar increase by about 75% for whites and by about 40% for blacks once these three variables are added to the model. However, it is really the first two variables that add most of the explanatory power; running a separate model without the *married-man* (1990) interaction term leaves the fit measures almost unchanged. Accordingly, we pay special attention to household composition variables—being married and having children—in our set-theoretic analysis.

To summarize, while the more complex model proposed by Fischer et al. clearly outperforms Herrnstein and Murray's model, neither of these logistic regression models is particularly successful at either correctly classifying those actually in poverty or at explaining variation in poverty outcomes. Given the fact that even the best model for white respondents misclassifies about 75% of those actually in poverty and fails to explain two-thirds of the variation in poverty outcomes, we believe that it is problematic to base strong policy recommendations on these results. While these models are able to show that factors such as parental income, being married, and gender clearly have an impact on the likelihood of being in poverty, their overall predictive power is severely limited and also differs substantially by subsample.

We turn next to a description of the independent variables used in our logistic regression analysis. These same variables are used as the basis for constructing fuzzy sets in our intersectional analyses.

The Middle Path: Independent Variables

After reproducing and evaluating Herrnstein and Murray's spare model and Fischer et al.'s elaborate model, we now offer a middle path between these models that focuses on only eight independent variables: race, gender, parental income, parental education, respondent's education, respondent's test scores, and respondent's household composition (marital status and dependents). As will become apparent, our middle-path model performs almost as well as the elaborate model of Fischer et al. but does so using only a small set of key variables, which we now discuss in more detail.

Race and gender. We conduct all our logistic regression analyses and intersectional analyses by both race and gender: black females, black males, white females, and white males are all examined separately, as different subsamples. While analyzing the net effects of race and gender in a model pooling the four subsamples would be interesting and useful, there are likely to be differences across race and gender in the effects of many of the independent variables included in the analysis. If we were to pool the four subsamples, we would then be required to test equations with three-way interaction terms (e.g., the three-way interaction between race, gender, and test scores). A more descriptive route to roughly the same analytic result is to conduct separate analyses by race and gender, as we do in the logistic regression analyses we present.

We should note that we study only two racial/ethnic groups, whites and blacks, and thus exclude Asian Americans, Hispanic Americans, and other minorities. The decision to exclude other minorities was based on practicalities (blacks and whites are the two largest groups in the NLSY), policy concerns (the black-white gap is the primary focus of the research literature on poverty), and substantive considerations (e.g., the obvious historical, political, and cultural significance of relations between blacks and whites in the U.S.).

Parental income. To assess parental income we use two measures from the NLSY: (1) the average of the reported 1978 and 1979 total net family income (the measure used by Fischer et al.), and (2) the official poverty threshold in 1979, adjusted for household composition in order to correct for the obvious impact of household size and composition on living standards. We divide net household income by the poverty level in order to create a relative measure of how far or close a given household is to being in poverty—our substantive outcome of interest. The resulting measure, the ratio of income to the poverty level, has multiples of the poverty level as its units. For example, a household with an income of $20,000 and a poverty threshold of $16,000 receives a score of 1.25 on our measure of parental income; a household with an income of $45,000 and a poverty threshold of $15,000 receives a score of 3.0; and so on. Households with incomes falling below the poverty threshold receive scores that are less than 1. Households with no income receive scores of 0.

Parental education. The NLSY reports both mother's and father's education in years. Rather than favoring one over the other, we simply use the higher of the two values. For example, if the mother had fourteen years of education and the father twelve, the resulting score for our measure is fourteen. In a two-parent household, the implication is that the impact of parental education on the respondent is shaped in large part by the parent with more years of education. This measurement strategy has the added benefit of yielding fewer missing values. In one-parent households, the score is simply the years of education of the single parent, regardless of the parent's gender. In households where the years of education value is missing for one parent, the resulting score is the level of education for the parent whose level is known.

Respondent's education. To measure educational attainment, the NLSY uses "Highest Grade Completed" (NLSY79 User's Guide, 1999, 138). This variable translates years of education directly into degrees (i.e., completing twelve years of education indicates a high school degree, while completing sixteen years indicates a college degree). Thus, there is a direct correspondence between the scores on this variable (measured in years) and degree completion.

Respondent's AFQT score. The AFQT scores used by Herrnstein and Murray are based on the Armed Services Vocational Aptitude Battery (ASVAB), which was introduced by the Department of Defense in 1976 to determine eligibility for enlistment. When we transform these scores into fuzzy-set membership scores (see chapter 4), we utilize criteria used by the military that is based on AFQT percentile scores. The military divides the AFQT scale into five categories. These five categories have substantive importance in that they determine eligibility for as well as assignment into different qualification groups. In order to maintain consistency with the scaling used in the fuzzy-set analysis, we use AFQT percentile scores in our logistic regression analysis. The correlation of the percentile scores with AFQT raw scores is .987; the correlation of the percentile scores with Herrnstein and Murray's normalized AFQT scores is .973.

Respondent's household composition. Household composition has two main components: whether or not the respondent is married and whether or not there are children present in the household. All four combinations of married/ not-married and children/no-children are present with substantial frequency in the NLSY data set. We code respondent's marital status as a dichotomous variable, assigning a value of one to those who were married in 1990. In general, married individuals are much less likely to be in poverty. While Fischer et al. use the respondent's actual number of children in 1990, we code "having children" as a dichotomous variable, with "yes" equal to one. The rationale for this is that being a parent imposes certain status and lifestyle constraints. As any parent will readily attest, the change from having no children to becoming a parent is much more momentous, from a lifestyle and standard of living point of view, than having a second or third child. In general, households with children are more likely to be in poverty than households without children. The most favorable household composition, with respect to staying out of poverty, is the married/no-children combination. The least favorable is the not-married/children combination.

Table 3.4 provides descriptive statistics, while table 3.5 shows the results of the logistic regression analyses for the four samples. As the tables indicate, our models are largely consistent with the findings of Fischer et al. Test scores consistently reduce the likelihood of being in poverty for all four samples,

Table 3.4 Descriptive statistics for middle-path models.

Variable	White males (n=1363)		White females (n=1315)		Black males (n=732)		Black females (n=775)	
	Mean	S. D.	Mean	S. D.	Mean	S. D.	Mean	S. D.
AFQT (percentile)	55.69	28.14	54.14	26.20	24.10	22.12	23.65	20.10
Parental income	6.89	4.06	6.92	4.17	3.41	2.81	3.20	2.88
Parental education	13.05	2.82	13.00	2.77	11.46	2.69	11.30	2.81
Respondent education	13.32	2.28	13.46	2.16	12.52	2.01	12.83	1.95
Married	0.59	0.49	0.65	0.48	0.36	0.48	0.35	0.48
Children	0.42	0.49	0.55	0.50	0.36	0.48	0.70	0.46
In poverty	0.06	0.23	0.09	0.28	0.18	0.38	0.31	0.46

Table 3.5 "Middle path" models. Logistic regression of likelihood of a person being in poverty in 1990 by race and gender.

	White Males		White Females		Black Males		Black Females	
	(1)	(2)	(3)	(4)	(5)	(6)	(7)	(8)
Intercept	1.527	2.927***	1.953*	2.945***	3.748***	4.291***	5.533***	6.477***
	(.971)	(.864)	(.993)	(.921)	(.863)	(.820)	(.926)	(.878)
AFQT (percentile)	-.021***		-.018**		-.016*		-.021**	
	(.006)		(.006)		(.008)		(.007)	
Parental income	-.151**	-.166***	-.051	-.063	-.121*	-.140*	-.121**	-.142**
	(.051)	(.051)	(.038)	(.038)	(.059)	(.058)	(.046)	(.046)
Parental education	-.036	.010	-.019	-.003	-.028	-.044	-.034	-.022
	(.056)	(.055)	(.052)	(.051)	(.044)	(.043)	(.040)	(.040)
Respondent education	-.212*	-.362***	-.256**	-.373***	-.340***	-.389***	-.480***	-.572***
	(.085)	(.073)	(.084)	(.074)	(.068)	(.064)	(.076)	(.070)
Married	-1.544***	-1.567***	-2.855***	-2.885***	-1.767***	-1.813***	-2.093***	-2.125***
	(.341)	(.332)	(.271)	(.269)	(.338)	(.337)	(.244)	(.244)
Children	.738*	.699*	1.745***	1.777***	.569*	.592*	.769***	.753***
	(.343)	(.332)	(.273)	(.271)	(.271)	(.270)	(.225)	(.223)
N	1363	1363	1315	1315	732	732	775	775
Pseudo R^2	0.182	0.164	0.329	0.317	0.173	0.167	0.286	0.277

* p < .05; ** p < .01; *** p < .001

but the effect is quite modest, with reductions in pseudo R^2 values of between .006 and .018 when test scores are excluded. We also find significant effects across the four groups for respondent education, being married and having children, again consistent with the findings of Fischer et al. In contrast, parental income reduces the likelihood of being in poverty significantly for all groups except white females. Lastly, our measure of parental education shows no discernible effect on the likelihood of being in poverty in our models, which is again consistent with the results of Fischer et al. In sum, our middle-path model indicates a very similar pattern of findings when compared to the main insights of Fischer et al.'s models, albeit with a substantially reduced number of variables.[5]

While these findings indicate that our reduced set of six variables occupies indeed an intermediate position between the underspecified model of Herrnstein and Murray and the overspecified one of Fischer et al., a comparison of the explanatory power of the subgroup models in fact allows us to trace differences in causal pattern across the four groups. Using pseudo R^2 values as a rough measure of explained variation, it appears that our models are best able to explain variation in poverty rates among white females (pseudo R^2= .329), followed by black females (.286). In contrast, the models perform significantly worse in predicting poverty among males, both white (.182) and black (.173). Our analyses thus show significant gender differences in the ability to explain variation in poverty rates, a finding not readily apparent in the results of Fischer et al. In their analyses, which are performed by racial category on a sample of males and females combined, adding a dummy variable for male respondents moves the pseudo R^2 values only from .168 to .185 for whites and from .183 to .213 for blacks, using estimates from our corrected models shown in tables 3.2a and 3.2b.

A similar yet even more dramatic difference between the subgroups emerges when using the percentage of respondents classified correctly as a measure of model performance, as shown in table 3.6. As the results for model 1 indicate, the subgroup regression for white males performs very poorly, managing to correctly classify only a single case (1.33%) of respondents actually

5. To create greater comparability to the results of Fischer et al., we also conducted further regressions (not shown here) in which we followed their approach of examining male and female respondents together but separating samples by race. Using this approach, the overall percentage of white respondents classified correctly in poverty in our model is 16.2% versus 25.79% in the preferred model A8 of Fischer et al., while for blacks the percentages are 43.65% in our model and 51.87% in Fischer et al.'s preferred model. This again shows how our relatively simple middle-path model performs only slightly worse than the much more expansive model of Fischer et al.

Table 3.6 Cases predicted correctly and incorrectly in subgroup models reported in table 3.5.

Observed cases	Cases not in poverty specified correctly	Percentage of cases not in poverty specified correctly[1]	Cases in poverty specified correctly	Percentage of cases in poverty specified correctly[2]	Total cases specified correctly	Overall percentage of cases specified correctly
Not in poverty: 1,288 in poverty: 75	whites males (n=1,363)					
Model 1	1286	99.84	1	1.33	1287	94.42
Model 2	1288	100.00	0	0.00	1288	94.50
Not in poverty: 1,200 In poverty: 115	whites females (n=1,315)					
Model 3	1178	98.17	41	35.65	1219	92.70
Model 4	1181	98.42	28	24.35	1209	91.94
Not in poverty: 600 In poverty: 132	black males (n=732)					
Model 5	587	97.83	17	12.88	604	82.51
Model 6	586	97.67	18	13.64	604	82.51
Not in poverty: 533 In poverty: 242	black females (n=775)					
Model 7	462	86.68	149	61.57	611	78.84
Model 8	460	86.30	151	62.40	611	78.84

[1] Number of cases not in poverty predicted / number of cases not in poverty observed.
[2] Number of cases in poverty predicted / number of cases in poverty observed.

in poverty. Removing test scores from the analyses in model 2 in fact improves rather than lowers the models' overall classification ability, albeit by correctly specifying two more cases not in poverty while no longer correctly specifying any respondent actually in poverty. The model naturally is again quite good at classifying cases not in poverty, but because it does misclassify practically all the cases that do experience poverty, the overall percentage of cases specified correctly is essentially identical to what one would have obtained by merely guessing that all respondents were not in poverty (94.50%).

At the other end of the continuum, our subgroup regressions perform quite well in classifying black females, as indicated by the results for models 7 and 8 in the table. For instance, model 7 classifies correctly 61.57% of black females actually in poverty—a huge contrast to the 1.33% of white males in poverty specified correctly in model 1. Here, removing test scores in fact slightly improves the percentage of cases in poverty classified correctly, albeit only by less than a percent and at the cost of lowering the percentage of cases not in poverty specified correctly. Furthermore, the predictive power of models 7 and 8 is also considerably better, as they correctly classify 78.84% of all respondents, as opposed to the 68.8% one would have obtained by a mere guess. The model thus reduces classification error by about a third (from 31.20% to 21.16%), which is sizeable considering that it accomplishes this with substantially fewer explanatory variables than the favored models of Fischer et al.

The remaining two groups—white females and black males—fall between these two extremes. For white females, the percentage of respondents in poverty classified correctly is 35.65% in model 3, while the same percentage is 12.88% for black males in model 5. In terms of a ranking of explanatory power, our subgroup regressions thus indicate that our models are best able to correctly predict poverty among black females (61.57%), followed by white females (35.65%), black males (12.88%), and white males (1.33%).

Conclusion

Our goal in this chapter has been twofold. The first was to reproduce the findings of Herrnstein and Murray and Fischer et al. in order to assure our further analyses using set-analytic methods are conducted on data consistent with that used by these authors. After showing that we are able to replicate their findings, we have set the stage for analyses applying very different methodological tools to essentially the same sample of respondents.

Our second goal was to begin probing the ability of prior models to tease apart the heterogeneity of causal paths towards a significant life outcome such as poverty. Here, we first showed that the models of Herrnstein and Murray perform rather poorly, while those of Fischer et al. do much better in terms of predicting poverty correctly, but at a considerable cost of parsimony. To strike a balance between these two approaches, we offered our own middle-path models that focus on only six relevant explanatory variables, examined separately by four subsamples based on race and gender. Our analyses demonstrated that there are in fact considerable differences among these subgroups of respondents. In particular, the analyses revealed that our models are able to predict poverty fairly well for black females, but hardly at all for white males, with the subgroups of white females and black males occupying intermediate positions in terms of our ability to correctly predict the occurrence of poverty.

Appendix: Correcting Fischer et al.'s Analysis

As we noted previously, in reproducing the results of Fischer et al. as reported in *Inequality by Design*, we encountered several problematic variables that we now discuss. The first problematic variable in Fischer et al.'s analysis is the dummy variable for men who were married in 1990. As reported by Fischer et al., this is an interaction variable for two other dummy variables (married in 1990 and male), both of which are significantly and negatively correlated with the outcome. Given this pattern of coefficients, it is frequently the case that the interaction term of two such variables is actually positive. However, the Married Man (1990) variable, as reported by Fischer et al., instead has a negative significant coefficient in the sample of white respondents. For the sample of black respondents, the Married Man (1990) variable also has a negative effect, but is not significant.

Using an interaction term for the *Married* (1990) and *Male* variables, we were unable to re-create these findings, regardless of whether we used the data provided by Arum or the original NLSY data. Rather, as might be expected, the interaction term for both variables was *positive* and significant. Only after reverse coding the dummy variable (i.e., coding 0 instead of 1 for married men) and after replacing the value of 1 with a value of 2 did we obtain results that closely match those reported in tables A2.3 and A2.4.[6] This leads us to believe that the results reported by Fischer et al. are due to a coding error and should not be interpreted as indicating that being married reduced the chance that a man was poor from 23 in 100 to 1 in 100 (Fischer et al., 1996: 90). Rather, as we show in our own corrected reproduction of

---

6. The coefficients and standard errors for the *Married Man* (1990) variable reported in models A8 and A9 in *Inequality by Design* are .506 (.181) and .534 (.180) for whites, and –.090 (.181) and –.101 (.180) for blacks (Fischer et al., 1996: 233–235). In models not reported here our own coefficients when using an incorrectly coded variable (reverse coded and assigned 2 instead of 1), are –.552 (.180) and .554 (.179) for whites and –.095 (.181) and –.112 (.181) for blacks, thus closely matching the results reported by Fischer et al.

the analysis, the interaction term somewhat reduces the additive benefits of being both male and married for white respondents.

The second problematic variable is the school composition measure introduced by Fischer et al. to capture the context in which respondents received their formal schooling. It consists of three indicators: the percentage of nonwhite students, the percentage of students who drop out of school, and the percentage of students who qualified for school lunches, which serves as a measure of economic disadvantage. All three measures were collected for the 10th grade of the last high school that the respondents attended. To create their school composition measure, Fischer et al. report that they standardized the three variables, summed them, and then divided by three. They also report that a mean value of 0 was assigned to missing school reports, and a dummy variable was added that was coded 1 for missing school reports (1996: 231).[7]

The fact that Fischer et al. use an index to measure attributes of the respondent's education is somewhat surprising, particularly since Fischer et al. themselves criticize *The Bell Curve* for using an index of parental socioeconomic status, which adds mother's education, father's education, occupational status, and family income. Specifically, Fischer et al. argue that lumping the different measures together in a scale would undermine the effect of parental income (1996: 77), thus leading Herrnstein and Murray to underestimate the importance of coming from a more affluent family background. Fischer et al. continue that "there is no statistical necessity for combining measures into indices, and there are often good reasons for looking at the measures separately" (1996: 77). We agree with this statement, and thus decided for our own analysis to disaggregate Fischer et al.'s school composition index. The appropriateness of disaggregating the index was also confirmed by a reliability analysis. For the white sample, the value of Cronbach's alpha was .46, thus suggesting that the school composition index had inadequate reliability. For the black sample, Cronbach's alpha was .58, a value that is slightly higher but still usually considered insufficient for an index (cf. Carmines and Zeller, 1979). Accordingly, we disaggregated the school composition index and included the three individual variables in our models.

7. Using mean substitution to address missing data is typically not recommended, as it tends to produce biased results (e.g., Little and Rubin, 1987). However, to maintain comparability to the analyses of Fischer et al., we do retain it in our reproduction of their results, but avoid it in our own middle-path models.

When using each component separately, a more detailed picture of the school environment emerges. For the white sample, a smaller percentage of dropouts as well as nonwhite students now has a significant negative effect, while the percentage of students that qualified for free lunches was not significant. However, given our general concern with effect sizes in these regressions, we will not elaborate on this finding here. For the black sample, none of the individual components was significant; this result is unexpected, since the coefficient for the overall index actually was significant and in the predicted direction. Still, given the inadequate reliability of the composite, we do not believe its use is justified.

Another issue with the school composite variable was that we were able to reproduce the results of Fischer et al. only by restandardizing the composite measure after a 0 had already been assigned to the missing cases. This is of course an incorrect way of proceeding. The correct way would have been to create the index only for cases where information on all three variables was available, standardize it, and only then assign a 0 to those cases where data was missing. Standardizing after 0s have been assigned to missing values distorts the variable and invalidates the method of using a dummy variable to control for the missing cases, since after restandardizing, those cases no longer have a 0 assigned to them and thus no longer fall along the mean. The result of this coding mistake is that the authors actually underestimate the size of the composite measure's negative effect. Still, this is a less important issue, since, as we have shown above, the composite measure is not an adequate measure to start with.

Finally, we encountered problems trying to re-create Fischer et al.'s measure of the unemployment rate in the local labor market in 1990. To create this variable, the authors stated they recoded a categorical NLSY variable into six values, ranging from 1.5 to 16.5 (1996: 232). However, the authors report a mean of 8.374 with a standard deviation of 5.699 for the sample of white respondents, and a mean of 7.180 with a standard deviation of 5.196 for black respondents (1996: 230). Our own analyses gave us means and standard deviations that were considerably smaller than those reported by Fischer et al.[8] Consequently, our regression coefficients for the unemployment variable do not exactly match those reported by Fischer et al., but we believe our results are in fact more accurate.

---

8. Our calculations gave us a mean of 5.590 with a standard deviation of 1.892 for the white sample and a mean of 5.121 with a standard deviation of 1.600 for the black sample.

FOUR

From Variables to Fuzzy Sets

Calibrating Membership in Sets

The first step in any set-analytic investigation, using either crisp or fuzzy sets, is the specification and construction of the relevant sets, including both the causal conditions and the outcomes. Three main phases in this process are: (1) the identification of the relevant causal conditions and outcomes, (2) the conceptualization of these conditions and outcomes as sets, and (3) the assignment of membership scores. With crisp sets, scores are either 1 (in the set) or 0 (out of the set). With fuzzy sets, scores range from 0 to 1, indicating the degree of membership of each case in a given set. When interval-scale variables are used as the basis for constructing fuzzy sets, the third phase involves specifying three empirical anchors that structure the translation of raw scores to fuzzy membership scores (see Ragin, 2008: chapter 5).

We base our set-theoretic analysis on the logistic regression analysis presented in chapter 3. Thus, the main causal conditions and the outcome are given; the number of cases by subgroup are 1,364 for white males, 1,315 for white females, 732 for black males, and 775 for black females. The outcome is poverty; the causal conditions are parental income and education, and the respondent's education, AFQT score, marital status, and presence/absence of children. The translation of these variables to sets involves an important reconceptualization of the underlying constructs. For example, "income" is easy to understand as a variable. However, in its "raw" form, it makes no sense as a set. The key difference between variables and fuzzy sets parallels the distinction between abstract nouns and adjectives. For example, "income" is an abstract noun, and abstract nouns make good variable names. Adding an adjective and creating "high-income," by contrast, distinguishes a specific category or range of cases and thus is a good starting point for constructing a fuzzy set. Another example: "education," an abstract noun, describes a variable; "college-educated," an adjective, describes a set.

The "variable/abstract noun" versus "set/adjective" distinction offers a good basis for understanding the second phase of calibration—the conceptualization of conditions and outcomes as sets. The set labels selected by the investigator should describe some case aspect that can be used as a basis for distinguishing cases in a qualitative manner (e.g., "high-income"). With crisp sets, the assignment of cases to sets is all or nothing—in or out. Fuzzy sets, by contrast, allow partial membership in qualitative states and are thus simultaneously qualitative and quantitative (Ragin, 2000: 153–155).

The third phase in the construction of sets is the assignment of membership scores to cases. With crisp sets, this assignment is usually straightforward. Distinctions that are conventionally understood as dichotomous (e.g., female/male) can be represented using 1s and 0s. While it is sometimes tempting to convert ordinal- and interval-scale variables to simple crisp sets, it is almost always a mistake to do so. Such forced dichotomizations often have an element of arbitrariness to them, which simply invites challenges. If an ordinal- or interval-scale variable exhibits variation that is meaningful to a set, as conceptualized and labeled by the researcher, then it is far preferable to capture this variation as degree of membership in a fuzzy set.

It is important to point out that the translation of interval-scale variables to fuzzy sets should never be mechanical, but instead must be based on substantive or case knowledge, with full attention to the conceptualization and labeling of the set in question. Basing set membership scores on such criteria as the range, the mean, the median, the rank order, or the standard deviation typically leads to fuzzy sets that are of questionable utility. Instead, the calibration of fuzzy sets must be rooted as much as possible in theoretical and substantive knowledge. This understanding of set membership scores justifies the conceptualization of membership assignment as a process of *calibration*, for the procedure involves the use of external standards and criteria to evaluate raw scores (Ragin, 2008:72ff).

When calibrating a fuzzy set from a source variable with a relatively small number of possible values (e.g., an ordinal-scale variable or a simple interval-scale variable), it is often best simply to assign membership scores to the original values using the recoding procedures that are built into most statistical software packages. For example, if the fuzzy set is degree of membership in the set of respondents who are college educated, then only a few of the values of the variable "years of education" come into play. For example, respondents with twelve or fewer years of education are coded as having full nonmembership in *college-educated* (fuzzy score = 0), while respondents with sixteen or more years of education are coded as having full member-ship in this set (fuzzy score = 1). Various levels of partial membership can then be assigned to respondents with 13 to 15 years of education.

More common in our analysis is the use of interval-scale source variables that are continuous (e.g., parental income) or that have many possible val-ues (e.g., AFQT percentile score). To calibrate these variables as fuzzy sets, we use the direct calibration method discussed in Ragin (2008: chapter 5). This method is based on the specification of selected interval-variable values as signaling (1) the threshold for full membership in the target set, which is translated to a fuzzy membership score of .95; (2) the threshold for full non-membership in the target set, which is translated to a fuzzy membership score of .05; and (3) the cross-over point, which is the dividing line between being "more in" versus "more out" of the target set, which is a fuzzy membership score of .50. The end result is typically an S-shaped curve, with low scores on the interval-scale variable approaching 0 and high scores on the interval-scale variable approaching 1.0. The calibration procedure is automated in the soft-ware package fuzzy-set Qualitative Comparative Analysis (fsQCA), based on the user's specification of the three benchmark values just described.

Why Calibration Matters

The central focus of set-theoretic analysis is the evaluation of subset and superset relationships. A fuzzy-subset relationship exists when the scores in one set (e.g., the fuzzy set of individuals with high AFQT scores) are consistently less than or equal to the scores in another set (e.g., the fuzzy set of individuals not in poverty). Thus, it matters a great deal how fuzzy sets are constructed and how membership scores are calibrated. Serious miscalibrations can easily distort or undermine the analysis of set-theoretic relationships. By contrast, for the conventional variable to be useful in a multivariate procedure such as multiple regression, it needs only to vary in a meaningful way. Often, the specific metric of a conventional variable is ignored by researchers because it is arbitrary or meaningless. After all, metrics disappear when correlations are computed, and matrices of bivari-ate correlations, or their mathematical equivalents, provide the foundation for many commonly used statistical procedures. For a fuzzy set to be useful, by contrast, scores must be carefully calibrated with respect to degree of set membership. Researchers must infuse their fuzzy sets with substantive knowledge, and membership scores must have face validity in relationship to the set in question and how it is conceptualized. A fuzzy score of .25, for example, means that a case is halfway between "full exclusion" from the set (a membership score of .0) and the cross-over point (.5—more in versus more out). This infusion of substantive knowledge comes primarily through the specification of empirical anchors based on external criteria. These empirical anchors guide and structure the assignment of fuzzy membership scores.

The central purpose of this chapter is to detail how we construct fuzzy and crisp sets from the middle-path variables we used in our logistic regression analysis in chapter 3. Thus, the main focus of this chapter is on the second and third phase of the process of constructing sets. The sets we discuss include degree of membership in the *two outcomes*, the set of individuals who are in poverty and the set of individuals who are not in poverty. Further, we discuss the degree of membership in sets reflecting various background characteristics and conditions: (1) respondents with low-income parents, (2) respondents with high-income parents, (3) educated respondents, (4) highly educated respondents, (5) respondents with educated parents, (6) respondents with highly educated parents, (7) respondents with low AFQT scores, (8) respondents with high AFQT scores, (9) married respondents, and (10) respondents with children. We also construct macro-conditions using these sets. For example, we use the intersection of respondents with *not-low-income-parents* and respondents with *educated-parents* to create the macro-condition *favorable-family-background*.

A few words are in order regarding the coding of related sets. For instance, the set of respondents *in-poverty* is the exact negation (also known as the complement) of the set of respondents *not-in-poverty*. Set-theoretic analysis is inherently asymmetric, and there is no guarantee that conditions linked to the presence of an outcome will be the reverse of those linked to its absence. Thus, it is important to conduct separate analyses of the conditions linked to poverty and the conditions linked to its avoidance.

The asymmetry of set relationships relates not only to conditions linked to an outcome or its absence, but also to different ways to create causal conditions of interest. This is helpful because it allows for slightly different causal conditions that in turn permit a more nuanced analysis of the evidence. For instance, the set of respondents with *low-income-parents* is *not* the exact negation of the set of respondents with *high-income-parents*, nor is the set of respondents with *low-AFQT-scores* the exact negation of the set of respondents with *high-AFQT-scores*. Parental income and AFQT scores are both calibrated in two different ways in order to permit examination of key differences in causal processes. For example, is it having *low-income-parents* that is linked to being in poverty, or is it having *not-high-income-parents*? By calibrating parental income to reflect membership in these two different target sets, it is possible to address this question using fuzzy sets. Likewise, is it having *high-AFQT-scores* that is linked to being out of poverty or is it having *not-low-AFQT-scores*? Again, by calibrating AFQT scores to reflect membership in these two different target sets, it is possible to address this question.

Poverty Status

To construct the fuzzy set of individuals in poverty, we use the official poverty threshold adjusted for household size and composition, the same measure used by both Herrnstein and Murray (1994) and Fischer et al. (1996). The official poverty threshold is an absolute threshold (National Research Council, 1996), meaning it was fixed at one point in time and is updated solely for price changes. It was first developed in the 1960s, based on the work by Mollie Orshansky and using the United States Department of Agriculture (USDA) economy food plan. After calculating the cost of this food plan for families of various sizes and compositions, the food expenses were multiplied by three to estimate the minimum total living cost and thus the official poverty threshold. This procedure was based on evidence from a 1955 household consumption survey, which indicated that the average family spent about a third of its income on food. While other poverty thresholds have been proposed, most notably by the National Research Council (1996), the official poverty threshold has the advantage of having been used extensively in prior research, and especially by the two studies that we have used as comparison cases for our own analyses. Furthermore, the official threshold correlates highly with the measure suggested by the National Research Council (1996).

NLSY data on the official poverty threshold includes two measures—poverty level and poverty status—both of which are based on official poverty thresholds (see NLSY79 User's Guide, 1999, 240–41). *Poverty level* is the level of income below which a family is considered to be in poverty, adjusted for family size, family composition, and state of residence. It is based on the yearly poverty income guidelines issued by the U.S. Department of Human Services and on Census Bureau poverty guidelines. *Poverty status* is a binary variable that gives the actual status of a family—whether family income is below the poverty threshold or not—and is calculated from information on poverty level and total family income for the past calendar year.

In their analyses, both Herrnstein and Murray and Fischer et al. use the poverty status variable as a binary dependent variable in logistic regression analyses. However, their dichotomous measure places families with

Table 4.1 Calibration thresholds and cross-over points for interval and ratio scale variables.

Fuzzy set	Source variable	Threshold for full nonmembership (.05)	Cross-over point (.50)	Threshold for full membership (.95)
In poverty	ratio of household income to poverty level for household	3.0	2.0	1.0
Not in poverty	ratio of household income to poverty level for household	1.0	2.0	3.0
Low-income parents	ratio of parents' income in 1978/9 to poverty level for household	5.5	3.0	2.0
High-income parents	ratio of parents' income in 1978/9 to poverty level for household	3.0	5.5	8
Low AFQT score	AFQT score expressed as a percentile	30th	20th	10th
High AFQT score	AFQT score expressed as a percentile	65th	80th	93rd

incomes just barely above the poverty level in the same category as families with incomes far above the poverty threshold, such as comfortably upper-middle-class families. Because it is based on a gradual membership function that better reflects the lack of clear-cut boundaries of a concept such as poverty (Neff, 2013), the fuzzy-set procedure avoids this problem. Our measure is based on the ratio of household income to the poverty level for that household. Using the direct method for calibrating fuzzy sets (see Ragin, 2008: chapter 5), the threshold for full membership in the set of households *in-poverty* (fuzzy score = .95) is a ratio of 1.0 (household income is the same as the poverty level); the cross-over point (fuzzy score = .5) is a ratio of 2.0 (household income is double the poverty level); and the threshold for full exclusion from the set of households *in-poverty* (fuzzy score = .05) is a ratio of 3.0 (household income is three times the poverty level for that household). The three qualitative anchors that structure our calibration of poverty status are listed in table 4.1.

The fuzzy set of households in poverty is a symmetric set; that is, it is truncated at both ends and the crossover point is set exactly at the halfway mark between the thresholds for membership and nonmembership. Thus, the set of respondents *avoiding-poverty* is based on a straightforward negation of the set of respondents *in-poverty*. With fuzzy sets, negation is accomplished simply by subtracting membership scores from 1.0 (see Ragin, 2008: chapter 2). That is, (*avoiding-poverty* membership) = 1 – (*in-poverty* membership). For example, a case that is mostly but not fully *in* the set of respondents *in-poverty*, with a score of .80, is mostly but not fully *out* of the set of respondents *avoiding-poverty*, with a score of .20. As we demonstrate in chapters 5–8, set-theoretic analysis is asymmetric in nature. Thus, the links between causal conditions and an outcome (e.g., the set of cases in poverty) must be examined separately from the links between causal conditions and the *negation* of the outcome (the set of cases avoiding poverty).

The use of a ratio of three times the poverty level for full membership in the set of cases not in poverty is a conservative cutoff value, but also one that is anchored in substantive knowledge regarding what it means to be out of poverty. For example, in 1989, the weighted average poverty threshold for a family of two adults and two children was about $12,500 (Social Security Administration, 1998: table 3.E). Three times this poverty level corresponds to $37,500 for a family of four, a value that lies just slightly above the median family income of $35,353 in 1990 (U.S. Census Bureau, Historical Income Tables—Families, table F-7).

There is no consensus within the scientific community on exactly where the poverty line should be drawn (National Research Council, 1996), and accordingly the question of who exactly is out of poverty is also subject not only to scientific investigation but also to value judgments. In fact, the National Research Council study suggested a poverty level that is between 14% and 33% higher than the poverty line in 1992. Against this background, our threshold of three times the poverty level for being fully out of poverty appears appropriate. Using a 33% higher poverty level, our threshold for *not-in-poverty* would translate to about double the poverty level.

Figure 4.1 presents a plot of degree of membership in the set *avoiding-poverty* against its source variable, the ratio of household income to household-adjusted poverty level. This figure illustrates the nature of the direct method of calibration. (To simplify the presentation, the plot is truncated at an income-to-poverty ratio value of 5.) Based on the threshold values shown in table 4.1, the direct method rescales interval or ratio scale variables so that they conform to the fuzzy-set metric, with scores ranging from 0 to 1. Note that once the threshold for full membership is crossed,

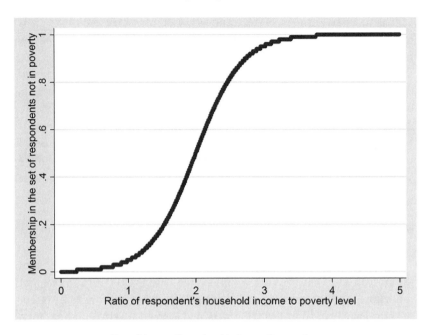

4.1. Plot of degree of membership in set of respondents not
in poverty against income-to-poverty ratio.

all raw scores are transformed to fuzzy-set scores close to 1. Likewise, moving in the opposite direction, once the threshold for nonmembership is crossed, all raw scores are transformed to fuzzy-set scores close to 0. This transformation of raw variation is consistent with the principle that set membership scores must reflect the labeling and conceptualization of the target fuzzy set. For example, the respondent whose household income is five times the poverty level is fully *not-in-poverty* and should be assigned a very high membership score in this set (i.e., 1.0 or virtually 1.0), as should the respondent whose household income is ten times the poverty level. In this way, membership scores distinguish between relevant and irrelevant variation, as dictated by the researcher's conceptualization and labeling of the target set and structured according to the threshold and cross-over values that the researcher specifies.

Parental Income

We assess parental income by first computing the ratio of parental income to the household-adjusted poverty level for the parents' household, as described in chapter 3. The numerator of this measure is based on the average of the reported 1978 and 1979 total net family income in 1990 dollars, the variable used by Fischer et al. to assess parental income. The denominator is the household-adjusted poverty level for that household. These data were used to create two fuzzy sets: the set of respondents with low parental income and the set of respondents with high parental income.

At first glance, it might seem redundant to calibrate two different fuzzy sets from the same source variable. After all, the logistic regression analysis uses only one variable—the ratio of parental income to household-adjusted poverty level. However, as we noted earlier, with fuzzy sets it is possible to explore nuances that are difficult to investigate using conventional quantitative methods. Consider, for example, the link between parental income and poverty avoidance. Is it respondents with high-income parents who are able to avoid poverty, or is it respondents whose parents are not low-income? In logistic regression analysis, these two questions are usually seen as one and the same, for the results of the analysis are expressed in terms of the change in the log odds of poverty for each unit increase in the measure of parental income. With fuzzy sets, however, these two questions are seen as separate, for the two sets in question have different labels and thus are calibrated differently. Consider the fact that full membership in the set of respondents with not-low-income parents does not guarantee full membership in the set of respondents with high-income parents. In fact, as we detail below, the threshold for full membership in the set of respondents with not-low-income parents (a membership score of .95), which is a ratio of income to poverty level of 5.5, translates to only .5 membership in the set of respondents with high-income parents.

We calibrate two fuzzy sets from a single source variable to account for the fact that we are interested in two different sets, with distinct labels: the set of respondents with *low-income-parents* (and its negation—the set of respondents with *not-low-income-parents*) and the set of respondents with *high-income-parents* (and its negation—the set of respondents with *not-high-income-parents*). By calibrating two fuzzy sets from a single source variable (the ratio of parental income to household-adjusted poverty level), we gain analytic leverage. This type of leverage is difficult to achieve using conventional quantitative methods because of the very high collinearity that often exists when the same source variable is used as a basis for two related independent variables (e.g., income and the log of income).

The fuzzy set of respondents with low-income parents is similar in its construction to the fuzzy set of households in poverty, described previously. That is, we first calculate the ratio of parents' household income to the poverty level, using NLSY data on the official poverty threshold in 1979, adjusted for household size and composition. Using the direct method of calibration, the threshold for full membership in the set with low parental income (.95) is a ratio of 2.0 (parents' income was only two times the poverty level). Respondents with ratios less than 2.0 receive fuzzy scores greater than .95. Conversely, the threshold for full exclusion (.05) from the set with low parental income is a ratio of 5.5 (parents' household income was 5.5 times the poverty level). Respondents with ratios greater than 5.5 received fuzzy scores less than .05. The cross-over point (membership = .50) is pegged at three times the household-adjusted poverty level.

Multiples of the poverty ratio (household income divided by household-adjusted poverty level) were also used to construct the fuzzy set of respondents with high parental income. The threshold for exclusion from the set with high-income parents (.05) is a ratio of three times the adjusted poverty level, the same as the value used for the cross-over point in the calibration of degree of membership in the set of respondents with low-income parents. The cross-over point (.50) was set at 5.5 times the adjusted poverty level, and the threshold for full membership was set at eight times the adjusted poverty level. The threshold for full membership corresponds roughly to three times the median family income, while the cross-over point corresponds to roughly two times the median family income. Again, the direct method of fuzzy-set calibration was used to calibrate degree of membership in this set (see table 4.1).

Constructing the set of respondents with high-income parents as multiples of the poverty ratio may seem odd, but our approach offers significant advantages. Most importantly, it allows us to take family size and composition (and thus financial need) into account, which is a significant issue if we want to be sure that our measure has substantive meaning across different household types. For example, an income of $70,000, or about two times the median family income, clearly should be considered high when assessing a two-person household (poverty threshold: $4,700; poverty ratio: 14.9), but may appear to be a lot less when assessing a seven-person household (poverty threshold: $12,300; poverty ratio: 5.7). Accordingly, respondents from the two-person household with an income of $70,000 have full membership in the set of respondents with high-income parents, while respondents from the seven-person household with the same income are just slightly more in than out of the set of respondents with high-income parents.

Respondent's and Respondent's Parents' Education

To measure educational attainment, the NLSY uses two variables, *highest-grade-attended* and *highest-grade-completed*. However, as Herrnstein and Murray

(1994: 599) and others have noted, respondents' answers to these two questions are not always consistent. Frequently, the degree does not correspond to the number of years of education. For a number of cases, for example, the highest degree ever received was reported as high school diploma, but the highest grade completed was far less than twelve. Furthermore, as these questions were administered every year, there were respondent-reported inconsistencies (Chuang, 1990). For example, *highest-grade-attended* and *highest-grade-completed* frequently decreased over time. To deal with these issues and construct a more reliable measure of high school and college graduation, Herrnstein and Murray (1994: 600) made several adjustments, such as requiring the highest grade completed to be within at least one year of the normal number of years required to obtain that degree. Using another approach, Fischer et al. did not tie the highest grade to a specific degree, but simply used the years of education completed before and after the respondent took the AFQT exam as their measure of education.

For the 1994 release of the data, the publishers of the NLSY conducted a major cleanup of the educational attainment section, with extensive recoding of the data to remove these inconsistencies. A new variable for "highest grade completed" was created (NLSY User's Guide, 1999, p. 132). This variable provides an improved measure of respondents' educational levels and furthermore translates years of education directly to degrees (i.e., completing twelve years of education indicates a high school degree, while completing sixteen years completed indicates a college degree). We use this improved measure of respondent's years of education to create our two fuzzy sets, degree of membership in the set of *educated* respondents and degree of membership in the set of *highly-educated* respondents.

Table 4.2 shows the translation of years of education to fuzzy membership scores for the two sets. Respondents with 12 or more years of schooling are more in than out the set of *educated* respondents (fuzzy score > .5). Those with fewer than 9 years of education are treated as fully out of the set of *educated* respondents (fuzzy score of .0), and those with 16 or more years of education are treated as fully in the set of *educated* respondents. The fuzzy set of *highly-educated* respondents was constructed by defining respondents with less than 14 years of education as more out than in this set. Based on this calibration, a respondent with 13 years of education is mostly in the set of *educated* respondents but mostly out of the set of *highly-educated* respondents.

As noted in chapter 3, we use the greater of mother's and father's years of education to assess parental education. In order to convert this variable to fuzzy sets, we use the same calibration scheme that we use for respondent's

Table 4.2 Calibration of respondent's and respondent's parent's education.

Years of education	Degree of membership in educated	Degree of membership in highly-educated
0–6	.0	.0
7	.0	.0
8	.0	.0
9	.1	.05
10	.2	.1
11	.4	.2
12	.6	.3
13	.7	.4
14	.8	.6
15	.9	.8
16–max	1.0	1.0

education. The two fuzzy sets for the parents exactly parallel the two just described for the respondents: degree of membership in the set of educated parents and degree of membership in the set of highly educated parents. The specific values assigned to the different years of parental education are shown in table 4.2.

Test Scores

There are two separate questions in the *Bell Curve* debate regarding test scores. The first concerns their validity: Do AFQT scores used by Herrnstein and Murray actually measure something that can be called "intelligence"? This question has generated a furious and seemingly endless debate (e.g., Herrnstein and Murray, 1994; Cawley et al., 1997; Fraser, 1995; Jacoby, and Glauberman, and Herrnstein, 1995). The second question concerns their utility: If AFQT scores are an acceptable measure of a generic, individual-level trait that is somehow relevant to success, how important are they in determining such life outcomes as poverty? In this study, we follow the lead of *Inequality by Design* in leaving the first question aside and focusing on the second question, which addresses the causal role of AFQT scores in the context of other relevant causal conditions.

The AFQT scores used by Herrnstein and Murray are based on the Armed Services Vocational Aptitude Battery (ASVAB), which was introduced by the Department of Defense in 1976 to determine eligibility for enlistment, an issue that had become prominent because of concerns over the quality of recruits as the United States moved from conscription to voluntary enlistment in 1973. The ASVAB includes 10 sections, 4 of which make up the AFQT, which is used to evaluate the general aptitude of service applicants: section 2 (arithmetic reasoning), section 3 (word knowledge), section 4 (paragraph comprehension), and half of section 5 (numerical operations).[1] In an effort to update enlistment norms, the ASVAB was administered to the respondents of the NLSY in the summer and fall of 1979. The NLSY respondents were chosen because they formed a nationally representative sample of young people born between 1957 and 1964. A total of 11,878 valid responses were obtained, and this sample was statistically weighted to be nationally representative. Following both Herrnstein and Murray and Fischer et al., it is on this sample that our subsequent analyses are based.

To construct our two fuzzy-set measures based on the AFQT, degree of membership in the set of respondents with high AFQT scores and degree of membership in the set of respondents with low AFQT scores, we rely on categories used by the Department of Defense to place enlistees. The military divides the AFQT scale into five categories based on percentiles. These five categories have substantive importance in that they determine eligibility for as well as assignment into different qualification groups. Persons in categories I (93rd to 99th percentile) and II (65th to 92nd percentile) are considered to be above average in trainability; those in category III (31st to 64th percentile) are considered about average; those in category IV (10th to 30th percentile) are designated as below average in trainability; and those in category V (1st to 9th percentile) are designated as markedly below average. To determine eligibility for enlistment, the Department of Defense uses both aptitude and education as criteria. Regarding aptitude, the current legislated minimum standard is the 10th percentile, meaning that those who score in category V (1st to 9th percentile) are not eligible for military service. Furthermore, those scoring in category IV (10th to 30th percentile) are not eligible for enlistment unless they also have at least a high school education. Legislation further requires that no more than 20% of the enlistees be drawn from Category IV, which further indicates that respondents in this category are substantially different from those in categories I to III.

---

1. The NLSY includes two measures of AFQT, called AFQT80 and AFQT89, that reflect changing calculation procedures used by the Department of Defense and are restricted to respondents who were at least 17 years of age. Neither Herrnstein and Murray nor Fischer et al. employ the AFQT scores provided by the NLSY, but instead use a slightly modified version of the AFQT that was recalculated using raw subtest scores for all 11,878 subjects for whom data was available (Herrnstein and Murray, 1994, 594n4; Fischer et al., 1996, 231). However, the difference between the Herrnstein and Murray variable and the AFQT89 variable is negligible, as the correlation between them is .987.

To construct the fuzzy set of respondents with *low* AFQT scores, we use respondents' AFQT percentile scores.[2] The threshold for full membership (.95) in the set of respondents with low AFQT scores was placed at the 10th percentile, in line with its usage by the military; respondents who scored lower than the 10th percentile received fuzzy membership scores greater than .95. The cross-over point (.5) was set at the 20th percentile, and the threshold for nonmembership was set at the 30th percentile, again reflecting the practical application of AFQT scores by the military. Respondents who scored better than the 30th percentile received fuzzy scores less than .05 in degree of membership in the set of respondents with low AFQT score.

The threshold for full membership (.95) in the set of respondents with *high* AFQT scores was placed at the 93rd percentile, in line with the military's designation of the lower boundary of their highest category; the cross-over point (.5) was set at the 80th percentile; and the threshold for full nonmembership (.05) in the set of respondents with high AFQT scores was placed at the 65th percentile, the bottom of the military's second-highest AFQT category.

It is important to point out that the military uses AFQT scores as a measure of trainability, not as a measure of intelligence. While similar in form and content to so-called intelligence tests, in actuality the AFQT and other such tests assess whether test-takers are able to recall the things that well-performing schools try to teach. Thus, the military's use of AFQT test scores as indicators of trainability is much more on the mark than their use as intelligence tests by Herrnstein and Murray, for the AFQT assesses not only recall of school material, but it also indirectly assesses both school performance and respondent's acquiescence to authority.

Household Composition

Household composition has two main components: whether or not the respondent is married and whether or not there are children present in the household. All four combinations of married/not-married and children/no-children exist with substantial frequency in the NLSY data set. We code

2. While Herrnstein and Murray state that they prefer using their heavily massaged AFQT *z* scores to using AFQT percentiles, they often resort to percentiles when presenting their descriptive evidence. The downside of using AFQT *z* scores is that the logistic regression results are skewed toward the relatively few cases that reside in the two tails of the AFQT distribution. In other words, the key contrast in Herrnstein and Murray's analysis is between the log odds of poverty for respondents with exceptionally high AFQT scores and the respondents with exceptionally low AFQT scores.

respondent's marital status as a crisp set, assigning a value of 1 to those who were married in 1990. In general, married individuals are less likely to be in poverty. While Fischer et al. use the actual number of respondent's children in 1990, we code *having-children* as a crisp set. The rationale for this is that being a parent imposes certain status and lifestyle constraints. As any parent will readily attest, the change from having no children to becoming a parent is much more momentous, from a lifestyle and standard of living point of view, than having a second or third child. In general, households with children are more likely to be in poverty than households without children. The most favorable household composition, with respect to staying out of poverty, is the married/no-children combination. The least favorable is the not-married/children combination.

Macro-conditions

Macro-conditions combine related case aspects. The creation and use of macro-conditions is motivated in part by substantive concerns and in part by methodological concerns. The usual substantive concern stems from the goal of bringing together multiple criteria for membership in a set. For example, a researcher might want construct a set that assesses the degree to which respondents are financially secure, with the latter defined as the combination of a good income and substantial assets. Using fuzzy sets, the calculation of degree of membership in the combination of these two sets is

$$(4.1) \qquad \text{financially secure} = \min(A_i, B_i),$$

where A_i is degree of membership in the set of respondents with good incomes, and B_i is degree of membership in the set of respondents with substantial assets. In order for respondents to receive a high score in *financially-secure* (i.e., close to 1.0), they must have high scores in both component sets. A low score in either set would result in a low score in the combination.[3] The practical methodological motivation for creating macro-conditions stems from the combinatorial nature of truth table analysis, a technique we use in chapters 7 and 8. All logically possible combinations of conditions are included in a truth table. For each additional condition, the truth table doubles in size. More precisely, the number of truth table rows

---

3. This use of logical *and* contrasts sharply with averaging the component scores. Using logical *and*, respondents are not able to compensate for low fuzzy membership scores in one component with a high membership score in the other. The lower of the two scores determines degree of membership in the combination.

is 2^k, where k is the number of causally relevant conditions. The larger the truth table, the greater the proportion of rows lacking empirical instances, and the greater the dependence of the analysis on the researcher's assumptions regarding such rows (Ragin, 2008:160–75). Thus, if it is possible to reduce the number of conditions by combining conditions that constitute coherent macro-conditions, it is prudent to do so.

In the analyses presented in chapters 7 and 8, we use two macro-conditions: *favorable-family-background* and *favorable-domestic-situation*. *Favorable-family-background* combines *not-low-income-parents* and *educated-parent* using logical *and* (intersection). Only respondents with high fuzzy membership scores in both component sets receive a high membership score in *favorable-family-background*. In effect, respondents with high scores in *favorable-family-background* constitute a subset of the respondents with *not-low-income-parents* and a subset of the respondents with *educated-parents*. *Favorable-domestic-situation*, by contrast, creates a single fuzzy set out of two crisp sets, *married* versus *not-married* and *children* versus *no-children*. The combination of these two crisp sets yields four different domestic situations that, in turn, can be arrayed in terms of the degree of protection they offer from poverty. The most advantageous is being married without children; the second most advantageous is being married with children; next comes not-married without children; the least favorable is not-married with children. Thus, the fuzzy set *favorable-domestic-situation* utilizes the following membership scores: married/ no children (1), married/children (.6), not-married/no children (.4), not-married/children (0).

Conclusion

This chapter describes how we calibrate our fuzzy sets using the variables examined in the logistic regression analysis presented in chapter 3. Our two outcome fuzzy sets, *in-poverty* and *not-in-poverty*, depart the most from their chapter 3 counterparts because they involve graded set membership, based on the ratio of household income to household adjusted poverty level. By contrast, the logistic regression analysis uses a simple dichotomous outcome, *in-poverty* versus *not-in-poverty*, a practice that equates respondents who are barely above the poverty threshold with those who are wealthy. By calibrating degree of membership in the set of respondents in poverty, we offer an approach that overcomes forced dichotomization and that is a much closer match with the way poverty is seen and understood in the larger society. There are many who are on the edge of poverty and are at great risk of falling prey to the pull of the reinforcing disadvantages and

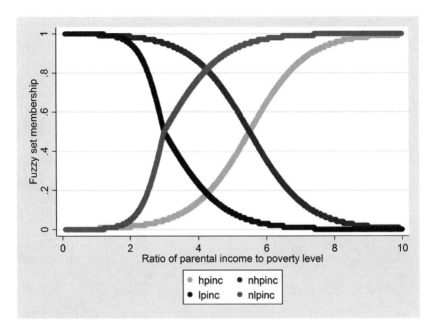

4.2. The four fuzzy-set calibrations of ratio of parental income to poverty level.

liabilities linked to being poor. Our fuzzy set captures not only those who are clearly in poverty, but also the partial membership of those who are on this precipice.

Altogether, we calibrate 8 fuzzy-set causal conditions, 2 crisp set conditions and 2 macro-conditions, a total of 12 conditions. To review, the fuzzy-set conditions are (1) respondents with low-income parents, (2) respondents with high-income parents, (3) educated respondents, (4) highly educated respondents, (5) respondents with educated parents, (6) respondents with highly educated parents, (7) respondents with low AFQT scores, and (8) respondents with high AFQT scores; the two crisp conditions are (9) married respondents and (10) respondents with children; and the two macro-conditions are (11) favorable family background and (12) favorable domestic situation. The 8 fuzzy sets are based on the 4 interval-scale independent variables we use in our logistic regression analysis in chapter 3. Each one of these 4 interval-scale variables is "double calibrated" to produce fuzzy sets addressing different substantive concerns.

Note also that all 12 conditions are examined in their original and in their negated forms (e.g., *un*favorable family background), which provides important analytic leverage. Figure 4.2 illustrates the different calibrations of

Table 4.3 Descriptive statistics for set membership scores.*

	Black females	Black males	White females	White males
Educated parent	.468 (.301)	.491 (.290)	.652 (.277)	.657 (.271)
Highly educated parent	.298 (.274)	.308(.266)	.475 (.335)	.476 (.330)
Low-income parent	.636 (.403)	.593 (.404)	.172 (.285)	.178 (.295)
High-income parent	.179 (.306)	.197 (.314)	.577 (.385)	.581 (.390)
Educated respondent	.656 (.228)	.620 (.244)	.724 (.224)	.703 (.239)
Highly educated respondent	.447 (.278)	.411 (.277)	.541 (.320)	.518 (.322)
Low test score	.539 (.424)	.537 (.437)	.122 (.280)	.145 (.312)
High test score	.023 (.112)	.035 (.149)	.218 (.345)	.254 (.369)
Married	.347 (.476)	.355 (.479)	.649 (.477)	.594 (.491)
Children	.703 (.457)	.361 (.480)	.554 (.497)	.420 (.494)
Favorable family background	.253 (.317)	.284 (.312)	.598 (.304)	.599 (.303)
Favorable domestic situation	.327 (.318)	.469 (.233)	.567 (.278)	.588 (.242)

*mean (standard deviation).

a single source variable, ratio of parental income to poverty level, into four fuzzy sets— *low-income-parents*, *not-low-income-parents*, *high-income-parents*, and *not-high-income-parents*. Four key contrasts can be exploited via these multiple calibrations of the same source variable: low-income versus not-low income, low-income versus not-high income, high income versus not-high income, and high income versus not-low income. Comparable analytic leverage is difficult to achieve using conventional statistical techniques because of their dependence on correlation and the calculation of net effects. For example, the correlation between low-income parents and not-high-income parents is .82, which would signal a potential collinearity problem in multiple regression and other popular statistical techniques.

Table 4.3 presents the descriptive statistics for membership scores in the twelve sets. The overall pattern is clear. With the exception of presence/absence of children, within-race gender differences are very small. More than 70% of black females have children, compared to 36% of black males. The comparable figures for whites are 55% with children for females and 42% with children for males. While within-race gender differences tend to be small, between-race differences are substantial. In essence, whites have much higher average membership scores in sets representing advantages (e.g., having high-income or highly educated parents), and much lower average membership scores in sets representing disadvantages (e.g., having low test scores or low-income parents). These racial differences are important. In chapters 5–8 we match whites and blacks according to their different combinations of advantages and disadvantages. As will become even more apparent, combinations of advantages are much more prevalent among whites, while combinations of disadvantages are much more prevalent among blacks.

As we noted at the outset, it matters a great deal how fuzzy sets are calibrated. Miscalibrations can seriously distort the results of set-theoretic analysis. In all our calibrations we have been guided by our substantive knowledge and interests, and we have searched the existing research literature for the guidance it offers. Without a doubt, dramatically different calibrations would produce different results. While some would consider this influence of calibration decisions "undue" and might portray this aspect of fuzzy-set analysis as a liability, we consider it a strength of the approach. Because calibration is important, researchers must pay careful attention to the definition and construction of their fuzzy sets, and they are forced to acknowledge that substantive knowledge is, in essence, a prerequisite for social scientific analysis.

FIVE

Test Scores, Parental Income, and Poverty

The data analysis presented by Herrnstein and Murray in *The Bell Curve* is surprisingly simple. Many observers describe it as "underspecified" (e.g., Heckman, 1995) because it is so lean, and this charge is in fact one of the main complaints lodged by Fischer et al., the research team that mounted the most extensive data-based challenge to Herrnstein and Murray. Most of the *Bell Curve* statistical analyses focus on two independent variables—test scores and parental socioeconomic status (SES)—and most of the analyses are little more than contests between these two variables, along with one or two perfunctory control variables (e.g., age of the respondent). This chapter also presents a relatively lean analysis, focusing on the main characters in the *Bell Curve* drama: test scores, parental background, and poverty. The key difference is that we set aside conventional quantitative methods and instead take advantage of the analytic nuance that can be gained using set-analytic methods and fuzzy sets. With this lean analysis in place, it will become much easier in subsequent chapters to add other causal conditions to the analysis.

We first address four questions concerning the impact of causal conditions considered one at a time: (1) Is there a connection between test scores and poverty? (2) Does this connection differ by race and gender? (3) Is there a connection between parental income and poverty? (4) Does this connection differ by race and gender? While these questions seem simple and straightforward, we conduct the analysis of the empirical evidence in a way that is in fact much more nuanced than is typical of conventional forms of quantitative analyses. Using set-analytic methods, this greater nuance is achieved by:

(a) separating the analysis of the outcome (*in-poverty*) from the analysis of its negation (*not-in-poverty*);

Table 5.1 **Hypothetical cross-tabulation of poverty by parental income: white female sample.**

	low-income-parents	*not-low-income-parents*
not-in-poverty	65	98
in-poverty	35	2

$N = 200$.

(b) examining not only the degree to which cases with a given causal condition consistently exhibit the outcome in question (the analysis of "shared outcomes") but also assessing the degree to which cases with a given outcome consistently exhibit the same antecedent conditions (the analysis of "shared antecedents");

(c) utilizing different conceptualizations of the causal conditions, which in turn provide the basis for different calibrations of set membership scores (e.g., the set of respondents with *high-income-parents* versus those with *not-low-income-parents*).[1]

In set-analytic assessments, it is standard practice to separate the analysis of an outcome (e.g., *in-poverty*) from the analysis of its negation (e.g., *not-in-poverty*). This separation is important because a causal condition may be consistently connected to one but not the other—that is, the combinations of conditions connected to the outcome may differ from those connected to its absence. While this aspect of set-theoretic analysis may seem odd from a correlational perspective, it is central to the intrinsically asymmetrical character of set-analytic approaches. For example, using set-analytic methods it is possible to show that white females with *not-low-income-parents* are consistently able to avoid poverty. However, the inverse connection between having *low-income-parents* and poverty, again for white females, is relatively weak.

For illustration, consider the hypothetical cross-tabulation of crisp sets shown in table 5.1. In the examination of outcomes, set-theoretic analysis divides this table into two parts, separating the columns. The strong connection between having *not-low-income-parents* and avoiding poverty contrasts sharply with the weak connection between having *low-income-parents* and experiencing poverty. The important observation in this example is that there is a highly consistent subset relation evident in the table: respondents with *not-low-income-parents* are able to avoid poverty; that is, they share this

1. Because set-theoretic analysis is asymmetrical, using different calibrations can have a substantial impact on the consistency of set-theoretic relations.

Table 5.2 Hypothetical cross-tabulation of poverty by domestic situation: white female sample.

	married or no children	unmarried with children
not-in-poverty	65	35
in-poverty	2	98

N = 200.

outcome. By contrast, respondents with *low-income-parents* do not consistently share the outcome of being *in-poverty*.

This example focuses on outcomes shared by cases with specific conditions. However, another feature of set-theoretic analysis that allows greater analytic nuance is its dual focus on shared outcomes and shared antecedents. Most applications of set-theoretic methods in the social sciences focus on cases sharing a given outcome, as just described (white females with *not-low-income-parents* consistently avoid poverty). However, it is possible as well to use set-theoretic methods to ask questions about shared antecedent conditions. Consider, for example, the question: Are white females in poverty a consistent subset of respondents who are unmarried with children? If so, then being unmarried with children may be considered a shared antecedent condition for white-female poverty.

The contrast between the analysis of shared outcomes and the analysis of shared antecedents is easy to illustrate using crisp sets. Table 5.1 above illustrates the analysis of shared outcomes. The focus is on the separate columns of the table (which specify the values of the causal condition), and how consistently the cases in a column share an outcome (e.g., as in the second column). Table 5.2 illustrates a hypothetical examination of shared antecedents: white females in poverty are almost uniformly unmarried with children. When examining shared antecedent conditions, the focus is on the separate rows of the table (which specify the values of the outcome), and whether there are any shared antecedent conditions (e.g., as in the second row of table 5.2).

These two features of set-theoretic analysis provide a basis for examining all four pairs of adjacent cells in a 2 × 2 cross-tabulation of a causal condition and an outcome, for each pair embodies a potentially relevant set relation. For illustration, consider table 5.3, which uses a generic cause (X versus ~X) and outcome (Y versus ~Y). (The "~"indicates negation or "not.") If the expectation is that the presence of X is linked to the presence of Y or that the absence of X is linked to the absence of Y, then there are four set relations to investigate:

Do instances of condition X share outcome Y? If so, then X should be a consistent subset of Y. The crisp-subset calculation is b/(b+d) or $\Sigma(X_i \cap Y_i)/\Sigma X_i$.

Do instances of condition ~X share outcome ~Y? If so, then ~X should be a consistent subset of ~Y. The crisp-subset consistency calculation is c/(a+c) or $\Sigma(\sim X_i \cap \sim Y_i)/\Sigma \sim X_i$.

Do instances of outcome Y share antecedent condition X? If so, then Y should be a consistent subset of X. The crisp-subset consistency calculation is b/(a+b) or $\Sigma(X_i \cap Y_i)/\Sigma Y_i$.

Do instances of outcome ~Y share antecedent condition ~X? If so, then ~Y should be a consistent subset of ~X. The crisp-subset consistency calculation is c/(c+d) or $\Sigma(\sim X_i \cap \sim Y_i)/\Sigma \sim Y_i$.

The examples shown in tables 5.1, 5.2, and 5.3 use crisp sets in order to simplify the presentation. The same principles and parallel procedures apply to fuzzy sets (with set membership scores ranging from 0 to 1), which are used extensively throughout this work. Comparable procedures are not part of the conventional multivariate analysis tool kit of most quantitative researchers today. These conventional techniques tend to emphasize the calculation of symmetric statistics summarizing an entire table or pattern of covariation. Set-theoretic analysis, by contrast, dissects relationships, providing greater analytic nuance and empirical specificity.

It is important to recognize that there are complementary connections among these assessments of subset relations. Suppose, for example, a researcher demonstrates that instances of condition X share outcome Y, that is, that instances of a causal condition constitute a more-or-less consistent subset of the outcome. The next question is: How common is the X•Y connection among instances of Y? That is, how much of the membership in Y is covered (or "explained") by X? This calculation is $\Sigma(X_i \cap Y_i)/\Sigma Y_i$. Note, however, that this calculation is the same as the calculation of the degree to which Y is a consistent subset of X (i.e., the degree to which X can be considered a shared antecedent condition for Y). The important point is that the same calculation has different meanings depending upon context.

Table 5.3 Hypothetical cross-tabulation of a causal condition (X) and an outcome (Y).

	~X	X
Y	a	b
~Y	c	d

Table 5.4 Evaluating the subset consistency and empirical relevance of set-theoretic connections.

Calculation	Primary use	Secondary use
$\Sigma(X_i \cap Y_i)/\Sigma(X_i)$	Evaluates the degree to which X is a consistent subset of Y (i.e., degree to which Y is a shared outcome)	If Y is a consistent subset of X (i.e., X is a shared antecedent), evaluates the empirical relevance of the connection
$\Sigma(X_i \cap Y_i)/\Sigma(Y_i)$	Evaluates the degree to which Y is a consistent subset of X (i.e., degree to which X is a shared antecedent for Y)	If X is a consistent subset of Y (i.e., Y is a shared outcome), evaluates the empirical relevance of the connection

If it is established that X is a consistent subset of Y, $\Sigma(X_i \cap Y_i)/\Sigma Y_i$ gauges the prevalence of the X•Y connection among instances of Y. If, however, X is not a consistent subset of Y (i.e., instances of X do *not* share outcome Y), then this same calculation can be used to gauge the degree to which Y is a consistent subset of X (i.e., the degree to which X is a shared antecedent condition for Y).

The complementarity of these set-theoretic assessments flows in the other direction as well. Suppose a researcher demonstrates that cases with outcome Y share X as an antecedent condition, that is, that instances of outcome Y constitute a more or less consistent subset of antecedent condition X. The next question is: How common is the X•Y connection among instances of X? If it is not very common, then the empirical relevance of X as an antecedent condition is low.[2] The calculation of the empirical relevance of a shared antecedent is the same as the calculation of the degree to which X is a subset of Y, $\Sigma(X_i \cap Y_i)/\Sigma X_i$. In the analyses that follow, once a highly consistent subset relation is established, the companion calculation is interpreted as a gauge of the empirical relevance of that connection. Table 5.4 describes the different uses of these two calculations and their complementary relation.

Further analytic nuance is gained using set-analytic methods by implementing multiple calibrations of the same source variable, as specified in

---

2. For example, suppose heroin addicts in the U.S. constitute a consistent subset of former milk drinkers. The empirical relevance of drinking milk as an antecedent condition (i.e., as a gateway substance) for heroin addiction is infinitesimal given that almost everyone is a former milk drinker. The set of former milk drinkers completely dwarfs the subset of former milk drinkers who are heroin addicts.

different verbal formulations of a given argument or proposition. For example, in order to avoid poverty, is it important to have *high-income-parents*, or is having *not-low-income-parents* good enough? To address such questions, source variables (such as parental income) can be transformed into two fuzzy sets (e.g., the set of respondents with *high-income-parents* and the set of respondents with *not-low-income-parents*) using different benchmark criteria for membership and nonmembership. Different criteria must be used because it is much easier for a respondent to have full membership in the set with *not-low-income-parents* than it is to have full membership in the set with *high-income-parents*.

In conventional quantitative analyses, questions of this type are often bypassed altogether because the focus is on causal conditions as "independent variables." The key questions asked of an independent variable are: Is its net effect significant? If significant, is the effect negative or positive? Does the independent variable explain a nontrivial proportion of the variation in the dependent variable? And how much does the dependent variable increase (or decrease) for each unit increase in the independent variable (e.g., for each \$1,000 of parental income)?[3] As we illustrate in the analysis that follows, how membership scores in sets are derived matters a great deal, and it is important for these scores to reflect as closely as possible the labels attached to sets.

The Connection between Test Scores and Poverty

The connection between test scores and poverty has been hotly contested ever since this issue was forcefully resurrected by Herrnstein and Murray in *The Bell Curve*. For these authors and their many critics, the central issue is one of net effects: Which is more important when it comes to important life outcomes such as avoiding poverty: parental SES or test scores? We set aside the question of "relative importance" for now and present a thorough interrogation of the connection between test scores and poverty. In the next section we examine the connection between parental income and poverty. In the end, we argue that the question of "relative importance" of test scores versus parental income is misguided.

---

3. Of course, conventional methods can be used to answer questions about thresholds (e.g., at what parental income level does the probability of avoiding poverty for respondents exceed .5?), but such questions are rarely asked. In any event, the answers to such questions depend on both (1) model specification and (2) the values of the other independent variables in the model.

Table 5.5 presents our set-theoretic analysis of test scores and poverty. Test scores are calibrated in two ways: (1) degree of membership in the set of respondents with *high-test-scores* (and its negation—the set of respondents with *not-high-test-scores*), and (2) degree of membership in the set of respondents with *low-test-scores* (and its negation—the set of respondents with *not-low-test-scores*). The outcome is poverty, which is operationalized as degree of membership in the set of respondents who are *in-poverty*, and its negation, degree of membership in the set of respondents who are *not-in-poverty*.[4] Altogether, there are four main analyses shown in the four panels of the table: (1) the connection between having *not-low-test-scores* and avoiding poverty, (2) the connection between having *high-test-scores* and avoiding poverty, (3) the connection between having *low-test-scores* and experiencing poverty, and (4) the connection between having *not-high-test-scores* and experiencing poverty. These four set-analytic connections are examined across four samples—black females, black males, white females, and white males. We examine not only whether cases with a given causal condition share the same outcome (reported in the first column of results), but also whether cases with a given outcome (*in-poverty* versus *not-in-poverty*) share the same antecedent condition (reported in the second column of results). The first column shows the degree to which the causal condition is a consistent subset of the outcome (shared outcome); the second column shows the degree to which the outcome is a consistent subset of the cause (shared antecedent). Because this analysis uses fuzzy sets (and not crisp sets as in tables 5.1– 5.3), the calculations are based on fuzzy membership scores and not simple counts of cases (see Ragin, 2008).

The first panel of table 5.5 examines the connection between having *not-low-test-scores* and avoiding poverty. The connection is strong for whites, but weak to very weak for blacks.[5] Notice also that for whites the connection works both ways—as a shared outcome (whites with *not-low-test-scores* consistently avoid poverty) and as a shared antecedent (whites who successfully avoid poverty consistently exhibit *not-low-test-scores*). In other words, it is

4. We use only one calibration of respondent income as the outcome, *in-poverty*, in order to maintain continuity with the prior research, which focuses explicitly on poverty as the outcome of interest. The calibrations of all the fuzzy sets we use in our analysis are described in detail in chapter 4.

5. In general, a consistency score of .75 is equivocal; .80 is adequate; .85 is good; and .90 and above is very good. The consistency calculations are based on sums of fuzzy membership scores, not on the proportion of consistent cases, and are descriptive in nature, not inferential (Ragin, 2008).

Table 5.5 Test scores and poverty: subset consistency calculations.

Sample	Shared outcome (subset consistency)	Shared antecedent (outcome coverage)
1. Not-low-test-scores → not-in-poverty		
black females	.691	.686
black males	.744	.572
white females	.801	.927
white males	.834	.898
2. High-test-scores → not-in-poverty		
black females	.919	.045
black males	.986	.057
white females	.919	.264
white males	.935	.299
3. Low-test-scores → in-poverty		
black females	.729	.734
black males	.519	.702
white females	.547	.276
white males	.440	.311
4. Not-high-test-scores → in-poverty		
black females	.546	.997
black males	.411	.999
white females	.285	.927
white males	.253	.919

clear that these two sets strongly overlap (i.e., they have a high degree of "co-incidence"). This high degree of set coincidence is illustrated in figure 5.1 with a simple Venn diagram. The intersection of the two sets occupies most of the area of their union.

The second panel of table 5.5 uses a different calibration of test scores—degree of membership in the set of respondents with *high-test-scores*. The results show that respondents who have *high-test-scores* consistently avoid poverty (the shared outcome), and this connection holds across all four race-gender samples. Taken together, the first two panels indicate that whites have a clear advantage when it comes to the connection between test scores and avoiding poverty. For blacks to avoid poverty, *high-test-scores* are required; whites are able to avoid poverty when they have *not-low-test-scores* (i.e., scores that are medium or better). While the subset consistency scores in the first column of the second panel are all excellent, it is important to note that the scores in the second column (i.e. relating to shared antecedents) are all very low. When there is a high consistency score for X as a

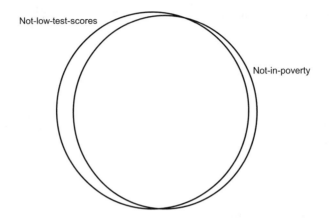

5.1. Venn diagram representing the connection between *not-low-test-scores* and *not-in-poverty* for white males: *Not-in-poverty* is .898 contained within *not-low-test-scores*; *not-low-test-scores* is .834 contained within *not-in-poverty*.

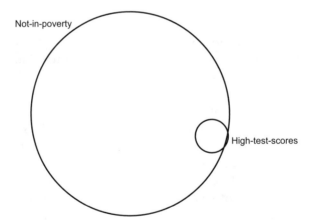

5.2. Venn diagram representing the connection between *high-test-scores* and *not-in-poverty* for black males: *High-test-scores* is .986 contained within *not-in-poverty*; *not-in-poverty* is .057 contained within *high-test-scores*.

subset of Y [$\Sigma(X_i \cap Y_i)/\Sigma X_i$] and a very low consistency score for Y as a subset of X [$\Sigma(X_i \cap Y_i)/\Sigma Y_i$], the results indicate that only a small proportion of the outcome (Y) is "covered" by the causal condition (X).[6] This pattern of results is comparable to observing that Harvard University graduates consistently avoid poverty, but they make up only a very small proportion of people who are not in poverty. In other words, while the connection between *high-test-scores* and avoiding poverty is clear, it is of relatively minor empirical importance relative to the total volume of poverty avoidance. The results for black males (from the second panel) are illustrated with a simple Venn diagram in figure 5.2. The intersection of the two sets occupies only a small area of the outcome, indicating that the causal condition (*high-test-scores*) accounts for only a very small proportion of the outcome (*not-in-poverty*).

The third panel of table 5.5 addresses the connection between having *low-test-scores* and experiencing poverty. While the subset consistency scores are stronger for blacks than for whites (the reverse of what was observed for the connection between *not-low-test-scores* and *not-in-poverty*), all the results are weak. None of the consistency scores in either column reaches .75, described previously as equivocal evidence in support of a fuzzy-subset relation. The fourth panel of table 5.5 shows that having *not-high-test-scores* is a shared antecedent condition for being *in-poverty*, a result that holds for all four race-gender samples. In other words, those who experience poverty consistently display *not-high-test-scores* (i.e., medium or low scores), regardless of race or gender. While the evidence of a connection between *not-high-test-scores* and experiencing poverty is clear, this finding must be qualified. When scores in the second column are strong, as they are in the fourth panel, it is also important as a next step to consider the evidence in the first column, the degree of consistency of X as a subset of Y.[7] If the scores in the first column are very low, as they are for whites, then the empirical relevance of the antecedent condition is also very low. Returning to the example of Harvard graduates: people in poverty may share the fact that they generally lack Harvard degrees, but if almost everyone lacks a Harvard degree, then the area of the superset (i.e., people lacking Harvard degrees) covered by the subset (i.e., people in poverty) will be low. As shown in panel 4 of table 5.5,

6. As explained in Ragin (2008), once it has been demonstrated that a causal condition is a consistent subset of an outcome, its coverage of the outcome (i.e., its empirical relevance) can be assessed by computing the quantity of the outcome that is covered by the causal condition.

7. As explained in Ragin (2008), once it has been demonstrated that an outcome is a consistent subset of a causal condition, the empirical relevance of the antecedent condition can be assessed by computing the quantity of the causal condition that is covered by the outcome.

the low-consistency scores in the first column for whites signal the relatively low empirical relevance of *not-high-test-scores* as an antecedent condition for poverty.

Overall, the evidence in table 5.5 indicates a substantial connection between test scores and poverty. This finding is consistent with prior research. While *high-test-scores* are linked to avoiding poverty and *not-high-test-scores* are linked to experiencing poverty, the strongest evidence of a connection between test scores and poverty is provided by the first panel, which shows that for whites there is a very strong two-way connection between *not-low-test-scores* and the avoidance of poverty.

The Connection between Parental Income and Poverty

Herrnstein and Murray (1994) compare the impact of parental socio-economic status (SES) and test scores on poverty. SES is an additive index based on parents' income, education, and occupational prestige. Fischer et al. (1996) convincingly demonstrate that the use of this index unnecessarily dilutes the impact of family background on poverty. They find that parental income by itself has a stronger impact on poverty than the SES index. We follow Fischer et al.'s lead and focus on the connection between parental income and poverty in our analysis.

Table 5.6 presents our set-theoretic analysis of the connection between parental income and poverty. Parental income is calibrated in two ways: (1) degree of membership in the set of respondents with *high-income-parents* (and its negation—the set of respondents with *not-high-income-parents*), and (2) degree of membership in the set of respondents with *low-income-parents* (and its negation—the set of respondents with *not-low-income-parents*). The outcome, as in table 5.5, is poverty, which is operationalized as degree of membership in the set of respondents who are *in-poverty* and its negation, degree of membership in the set of respondents who are *not-in-poverty*. Altogether, there are four main analyses: (1) the connection between having *not-low-income-parents* and avoiding poverty, (2) the connection between having *high-income-parents* and avoiding poverty, (3) the connection between having *low-income-parents* and poverty, and (4) the connection between having *not-high-income-parents* and poverty. As in table 5.5, we examine not only whether cases with a given causal condition share the same outcome (the first column of results), but also whether cases with the outcome in question (*in-poverty* versus *not-in-poverty*) share the antecedent condition (reported in the second column of results).

Table 5.6 Parental income and poverty.

Sample	Shared outcome (subset consistency)	Shared antecedent (outcome coverage)
1. Not-low-income-parents → not-in-poverty		
black females	.692	.541
black males	.741	.500
white females	.807	.880
white males	.847	.876
2. High-income-parents → not-in-poverty		
black females	.767	.295
black males	.833	.272
white females	.851	.647
white males	.889	.649
3. Low-income-parents → in-poverty		
black females	.665	.790
black males	.492	.735
white females	.470	.335
white males	.446	.387
4. Not-high-income-parents → in-poverty		
black females	.601	.922
black males	.453	.917
white females	.367	.643
white males	.336	.686

Overall, the results for parental income and poverty parallel the results for test scores and poverty. In the first panel of table 5.6 there is a very strong connection between *not-low-income-parents* and avoiding poverty for whites but not for blacks. Not only is the avoidance of poverty a shared outcome for whites with *not-low-income-parents*, but whites who avoid poverty also share *not-low-income-parents* as an antecedent condition. These results indicate a strong pattern of inheritance of advantage for whites. Blacks are not so lucky. The second panel of table 5.6 shows that black male respondents with *high-income-parents* are able to avoid poverty, although the results are equivocal for black females. For blacks, the low scores in the second column signal that the coverage of *not-in-poverty* by *high-income-parents* is low, which in turn indicates that it is not a common route to poverty avoidance for blacks. As with *high-test-scores* and avoiding poverty, having *high-income-parents* is not a common respondent attribute among blacks. It follows that this antecedent condition is not widely shared among blacks who avoid poverty. The more general lesson from the first two panels of table 5.6 is that for whites to avoid poverty, it is enough to have parents who are at least middle income; in contrast, for blacks it takes *high-income-parents* and the *high-income-parent* route is not nearly as common as it is among whites.

The third panel of table 5.6 shows only weak results for the connection between *low-income-parents* and experiencing poverty. This finding parallels the weak results in panel 3 of table 5.5. Moving to the fourth panel, it is clear that blacks who are *in-poverty* share *not-high-income-parents* as an antecedent condition, indicating a strong pattern of inheritance of disadvantage. The paired scores in the first column indicate that this antecedent condition is at least moderate in its empirical relevance, especially for black females. These results for blacks parallel their table 5.5, panel 3 results. Whites, by contrast, do not share *not-high-income-parents* as an antecedent condition for poverty, indicating a substantially lower degree of inherited disadvantage.

Overall, the analysis of the connection between parental income and poverty indicates substantial inheritance of advantage for whites, while blacks experience substantial inheritance of disadvantage. Note further that our set-theoretic analysis of shared outcomes and shared antecedents allows for a much more fine-grained analysis of the relationship between test scores, parental income, and poverty than would be possible with a conventional correlational analysis. We will return to this issue in more detail below.

The Confounding of Test Scores and Parental Income

Tables 5.5 and 5.6 present several parallel findings, for example, the strong set-theoretic connection for whites between *not-low-test-scores* and avoiding poverty in table 5.5 and the parallel connection for *not-low-income-parents* and avoiding poverty in table 5.6. These and other parallel findings suggest that there may be a substantial overlap in the impact of these two causal conditions on poverty. This leads to our next question: to what degree are these two conditions confounded with each other? This question is important for the simple reason that much of the *Bell Curve* debate has centered on the relative importance of test scores versus family background. If there is serious confounding between the two causal conditions, then it may not be suitable to try to assess their relative importance. Such an assessment also would divert attention from the much more important examination of the combined impact of the two causal conditions. In this section we contrast the set-analytic approach to the question of confounding with a conventional correlational approach. In the next section we examine the overlap in their effects on poverty.

Table 5.7 The correlation of test percentile score with the ratio of parental income to household poverty level.

Sample	Correlation	Correlation^2
black females	.382	.146
black males	.377	.142
white females	.299	.089
white males	.292	.085
pooled sample	.460	.212

The conventional way of addressing the question of confounded causes is to assess the degree of correlation between the two causes using statistics such as Pearson's r. Squaring this correlation shows the proportion of shared variance. If the proportion of variance that two variables share is substantial, then there is little to be gained from trying to estimate their separate effects or to try to use this information to determine which variable is more important. Table 5.7 reports the correlations between test scores (using percentile scores) and parental income (the ratio of parental household income to household poverty level) for the four race-gender samples and for the four samples pooled together.[8] The correlations are all modest, ranging from .292 for white males to .382 for black females to .460 for the pooled sample. The squared correlations, which range from .085 to .146 for the four race-gender samples, indicate that there is little shared variance and therefore little or no confounding. Thus, from the perspective of conventional correlational methods, collinearity is not an issue with these data, and researchers are free to estimate the separate effects of these "independent" variables on outcomes such as poverty. In short, there appears to be a solid basis for conducting the "contest" between independent variables presented by Herrnstein and Murray and also by their many critics.

However, correlations are symmetrical summary statistics, and they sometimes mask as much as they reveal (Ragin, 2008). As an alternative, we offer a set-theoretic analysis of the confounding of test scores and parental income. Specifically, we show that set-theoretic methods provide much greater analytic nuance. For example, set-theoretic methods can separate the analysis of the degree to which *high-test-scores* and *high-income-parents*

8. These two variables, which are the source variables for the fuzzy-set causal conditions used in this chapter, are described in chapters 3 and 4.

go together from the analysis of the degree to which *low-test-scores* and *low-income-parents* go together. Both analyses focus on substantively different issues: the first analysis addresses the degree to which advantages overlap and reinforce; the second addresses the degree to which disadvantages overlap and reinforce. By conducting these analyses by sample, it is possible to assess the degree of overlapping advantages versus overlapping disadvantages for the four race-gender samples. This type of analysis is beyond the reach of conventional correlation-based quantitative methods.

From a set-analytic perspective, the key issue in the analysis of causal conditions that are confounded is not their degree of correlation, but the degree to which the relevant sets in question have overlapping memberships. For example, to what degree is the set of respondents with *high-test-scores* the same as the set of respondents with *high-income-parents*? To answer questions of this type, we calculate the degree to which the memberships in the sets in question coincide—their degree of "set coincidence." Our measure of set coincidence is also known as a Jaccard coefficient, a similarity measure commonly used in the study of social networks. Its calculation is straightforward: for two crisp sets, degree of coincidence is simply the number of cases that reside in both sets (i.e., set intersection) divided by the number of cases that reside in either set (i.e., set union). The set coincidence of "religious fundamentalist" and "Republican," for example, is the number of people who are both fundamentalist and Republican divided by the number of people who are in either set. With fuzzy sets, the calculation of the coincidence of sets A and B is parallel to the crisp-set calculation:

$$\text{set coincidence } (A,B) = \Sigma(A_i \cap B_i)/\Sigma(A_i \cup B_i)$$
$$= \Sigma\min(A_i,B_i)/\Sigma\max(A_i,B_i).$$

Set coincidence scores range from 0 to 1; the score of 0 indicates no overlap; a score of 1 indicates that the two sets are identical. With fuzzy sets, a set coincidence score of 1 indicates that $A_i = B_i$, that is, the membership scores in one set are exactly equal to the membership scores in the other set for each case.

Table 5.8 presents the results of our analysis of the coincidence of test scores and parental income. We examine the coincidence of (1) *not-low-test-scores* with *not-low-income-parents*, (2) *high-test-scores* with *high-income-parents*, (3) *low-test-scores* with *low-income-parents*, and (4) *not-high-test-scores* with *not-high-income-parents* for our four race-gender samples. The first two analyses assess the degree to which advantages coincide; the second two analyses assess the degree to which disadvantages coincide. Further, using four different codings for each source variable (i.e. low, not-high, not-low, high) provides an

Table 5.8 The set coincidence of test scores and parental income.

Sample	Set coincidence
1. not-low-test-scores, not-low-income-parents	
black females	.421
black males	.418
white females	.792
white males	.788
2. high-test-scores, high-income-parents	
black females	.074
black males	.098
white females	.263
white males	.293
3. low-test-scores, low-income-parents	
black females	.555
black males	.520
white females	.195
white males	.239
4. not-high-test-scores, not-high-income-parents	
black females	.824
black males	.806
white females	.444
white males	.438

additional level of detail that allows us to determine with greater specificity how advantages and disadvantages are confounded by race and gender.

The first panel shows that there is a very strong set coincidence of *not-low-test-scores* and *not-low-income-parents* for whites (with set coincidence scores of about .80) but not for blacks (with set coincidence scores of about .40). In other words, white respondents who have *not-low-test-scores* tend to have *not-low-income-parents*, and vice versa, and the level of overlap between these two attributes is almost twice that of blacks. In practical terms, this result shows that (1) whites tend to combine these two advantages, and (2) for whites at least, it would be hazardous to try to separate the impact of these two conditions on membership in the set of respondents who are *not-in-poverty*.

The second panel shows a relatively weak coincidence of *high-test-scores* and *high-income-parents*. While set coincidence scores are stronger for whites than for blacks, again indicating that whites have more combined advantages, the degree of set coincidence is low (less than .3 for whites and less than .1 for blacks). The third panel shows very low coincidence of low-test-scores and low-income-parents for whites (with set coincidence scores of about .20) and a moderate level of set coincidence for blacks (with set coincidence scores over .50). These results indicate that blacks tend to suffer combined disadvantages more than whites, a pattern that is dramatically reinforced by the results shown in the next panel. Specifically, panel four shows a very high level of set coincidence of not-high-test-scores and not-high-income-parents for blacks (with coincidence scores greater than .80) and only a modest level for whites (with coincidence scores in the .40 range). Thus, blacks who have not-high-test-scores tend to have not-high-income-parents, and vice versa; that is, they display a much higher level of combined disadvantages than whites. The panel four results also indicate that for the sample of blacks it would be hazardous to try to separate the impact of these two conditions, not-high-test-scores and not-high-income-parents, on poverty.

To summarize: table 5.8 demonstrates that (1) whites enjoy combined advantages, while blacks bear the burden of combined disadvantages, and (2) test scores and parental income are highly confounded via set coincidence, as shown in two race-specific patterns (in the first and fourth panels of table 5.8). We demonstrate both racial differences and a very high level of confounding of these two causal conditions by separating the analysis of combined advantages from the analysis of combined disadvantages and by exploring different set-theoretic formulations of these measures. Note that the differences between blacks and whites we just demonstrated using set-theoretic analysis are not visible in an analysis using standard correlational tools. We turn next to the analysis of their overlapping effects on poverty.

The Intersectional Impact of Test Scores and Parental Income on Poverty

It is reasonable to speculate that the confounding of test scores and parental income shown in table 5.8 explains the parallel results shown in tables 5.5 and 5.6. Recall that table 5.5 shows that having not-low-test-scores and avoiding poverty are strongly linked for whites, while table 5.6 shows that having not-low-income-parents follows the same pattern, again for whites. In both tables the set-theoretic connection works both ways, as a shared-outcome connection (avoiding poverty) and as shared-antecedent connection (not-low-test-scores and not-low-income-parents). The other parallel findings from tables 5.5 and 5.6 concern blacks. Table 5.5 shows that having not-high-test-scores is a shared-antecedent connection for blacks who are in-poverty, while table 5.6 shows that having not-high-income-parents follows the same pattern. The corroboration of these parallel findings comes in table 5.8, which shows a high degree of set coincidence of *not-low-test-scores* and *not-low-income-parents* for whites and a high degree of set coincidence of *not-high-test-scores* and *not-high-income-parents* for blacks.

With set-theoretic methods it is possible to conduct an explicit assessment of the degree to which the effects of these two conditions on poverty overlap. The key is to compare the strength of the set-theoretic connection between the outcome and two individual causal conditions considered *separately*, on the one hand, with the strength of the set-theoretic connection between the outcome and the *intersection* of these two conditions, on the other. The intersection of two fuzzy sets is simple to calculate, as it is the minimum degree of membership across both sets:[9]

$$A \cap B = \min(A_i, B_i)$$

When comparing the strength of set-analytic connections, it is important to consider not only the degree to which cases with the causal conditions share the outcome (i.e., subset consistency), but also the degree to which cases with the outcome share the antecedent conditions (i.e., outcome coverage), as sketched in table 5.4. If there is considerable overlap in the effects of two causal conditions, then both subset consistency and outcome coverage will be about the same for their intersection as it is for the two causal conditions considered separately. When the overlap in their effects is very strong, then the effect that is observed separately for each causal condition is actually due to their *combination*, masquerading as the effect of a single condition. In other words, the results shown for the two causal conditions analyzed separately may be due to the fact that these two causal conditions have a very high degree of set coincidence. Thus, while it may appear that the two connections to the outcome are separate, they are in fact virtually one and the same.

Table 5.9 shows the results of the analysis of the overlapping effects of *not-low-test-scores* and *not-low-income-parents* on *not-in-poverty* for white males and white females. As expected, it is clear that the impact of these two causal conditions on *not-in-poverty* is very much an intersectional impact. The two ways of assessing set-theoretic connections (shared outcomes and shared antecedents) show that the results for the intersection of the two conditions are very close to the results for the two causal conditions considered separately. For white females, the subset consistency scores for the two conditions considered separately are .801 and .807; the parallel measure for their

---

9. In other words, for each case use the lower of the two fuzzy membership scores as the degree of membership in the intersection (the combination is only as strong as its weakest link).

intersection is .833. The outcome coverage scores for this same sample are .927 and .880 for the two conditions considered separately, and .828 for their intersection. The results for white males parallel the results for white females. These findings support our contention that whites enjoy combined advantages, and these combined advantages, in turn, are linked to their successful avoidance of poverty.

Turning now to the findings for black females and black males, table 5.10 shows the results of the analysis of the overlapping effects of *not-high-test-scores* and *not-high-income-parents* on experiencing poverty. The results for the intersection of the two conditions are again very close to the results for the two causal conditions considered separately. For black females, the subset consistency scores are .546 and .601 for the two conditions considered separately; the parallel measure for their intersection is .606. The shared antecedent scores for this same sample are .997 and .992 for the two conditions considered separately, and .920 for their intersection. The results for black males parallel the results for black females. The strong connections to *in-poverty* observed separately for the two causal conditions are due to the fact that they are strongly linked empirically. Thus, they should be considered jointly and not treated as separate or "independent."

Substantively, the results indicate that blacks in poverty suffer combined disadvantages as antecedent conditions. The same is not true for whites (see table 5.6, panel 4). In addition, note that the analysis for blacks shows that blacks experiencing poverty are an almost perfect subset of blacks exhibiting the two antecedent conditions of *not-high-test-scores* and *not-high-parental-income* (the shared antecedent scores shown in the second column of table 5.10). However, experiencing these antecedents does not uniformly lead to the shared outcome, as indicated by the relatively low subset consistency scores

Table 5.9 Overlapping effects of not-low-test-score and not-low-income-parents on not-in-poverty: white sample.

Sample	Condition	Shared outcome (subset consistency)	Shared antecedent (outcome coverage)
white females	not-low-test-scores	.801	.927
	not-low-income-parents	.807	.880
	intersection	.833	.828
white males	not-low-test-scores	.834	.898
	not-low-income-parents	.847	.876
	intersection	.863	.803

Table 5.10 Overlapping effects of not-high-test-scores and not-high-income-parents on in-poverty: black sample.

Sample	Condition	Shared outcome (subset consistency)	Shared antecedent (outcome coverage)
black females	not-high-test-scores	.546	.997
	not-high-income-parents	.601	.922
	intersection	.606	.920
black males	not-high-test-scores	.411	.999
	not-high-income-parents	.453	.917
	intersection	.461	.917

(the shared outcome scores shown in the first column of table 5.10). In other words, while almost all blacks in poverty come from those who exhibit both *not-high-test-scores* and *not-high-income-parents*, not all of those who exhibit these disadvantages end up in poverty.

Conclusion

The *Bell Curve* debate focuses almost exclusively on the relative impact of test scores versus family background on life outcomes such as poverty. For the most part, researchers engaged in this debate have all used the same analytic techniques, designed to estimate the net effects of independent variables lined up together in a contest to explain variation in a dependent variable. The correlational foundation of these techniques, however, is poorly suited to the examination of the subtle patterns we document in this chapter. The set-analytic methods we use allow much greater nuance. Their inherent asymmetry makes it possible to (1) separate the analysis of the conditions linked to an outcome from the analysis of the conditions linked to its absence, (2) separate the analysis of the degree to which cases with specific conditions share outcomes from the analysis of the degree to which cases with the same outcome share antecedent conditions, and (3) separate the examination of combined advantages from the analysis of combined disadvantages. On top of these benefits, we gain further analytic leverage by implementing multiple calibrations of the two causal conditions and conducting all our analyses by race and gender.

Our results demonstrate that it is hazardous to try to separate the effects of test scores and parental income on poverty—that it is unwise to treat the analysis of their effects on poverty as a contest. Whites combine advantages, and their combined advantages give them an important edge when it comes to avoiding poverty. By contrast, blacks tend to combine disadvantages, and their combined disadvantages are linked to their experience of poverty. This chapter demonstrates that by using techniques that allow more complexity and greater analytic nuance than offered by conventional methods, it can be demonstrated that the core of the *Bell Curve* debate is in fact misdirected. Rather than trying to prove that test scores or family background is more important for life outcomes, and generating a lot of ideological sound and fury in the process, researchers should focus instead on core questions in the study of inequality. These core questions center on the analysis of how individuals gain leverage by combining advantages and how they lose traction when disadvantages coincide.

SIX

Coinciding Advantages versus
Coinciding Disadvantages

In this chapter we offer an extended examination of coinciding advantages and disadvantages. The main focus is on the assessment of *multiple* advantages versus *multiple* disadvantages and the consequences of these coinciding conditions for experiencing versus avoiding poverty. While conventional multivariate techniques are capable of assessing multiple conditions, the usual goal of these techniques is to isolate each "independent" variable's separate or "net" impact on a dependent variable. The techniques we use, by contrast, focus on combinations of conditions and examine their intersectional impact. Furthermore, we conduct all our analyses by race and gender in order to highlight the varied manifestations and consequences of overlapping inequalities for four race/gender samples: black females, black males, white females, and white males.

In chapter 5 we show that whites tend to share two important advantages—*not-low-test-scores* and *not-low-income-parents*, while blacks tend to share two disadvantages—*not-high-test-scores* and *not-high-income-parents*. Moreover, these combined traits are linked to poverty, and the consistency of these links varies consistently and dramatically by race. Whites who share the two advantages consistently avoid poverty, while blacks in poverty consistently share the two disadvantages as antecedent conditions. The analyses presented in this chapter build on the findings presented in chapter 5 in two ways: first, we extend the examination of coinciding inequalities that we began in the previous chapter to include additional conditions. Specifically, we supplement the two conditions featured in chapter 5 (test scores and parental income) with fuzzy sets based on respondent's years of education and respondent's parents' years of education—two of the key factors we

identified in chapter 3.[1] Using fuzzy-set-analytic methods, this analysis focuses on the degree to which multiple advantages and multiple disadvantages coincide. Second, we turn to an examination of the consequences of
overlapping inequalities for poverty. How strong is the link between overlapping advantages and the avoidance of poverty, and does the consistency
of this connection differ by race and gender? How strong is the link between
overlapping disadvantages and poverty, and does the strength of this connection differ by race and gender?

Our results show that the link between multiple advantages and avoiding poverty is much more consistent than the link between multiple disadvantages and experiencing poverty. Substantively, this finding suggests that
the variables conventionally used to study poverty are more relevant to understanding how the accumulation of advantages shields people from poverty. They are less relevant to understanding how people succumb to or are
locked into poverty due to their multiple disadvantages.[2] This asymmetry
cannot be detected using conventional quantitative methods because these
methods are based directly or indirectly on symmetric correlational reasoning. As we discuss in subsequent chapters, this difference in the ability to
understand what leads people to avoid poverty versus what leads people to
end up in poverty carries important consequences for the process of creating
policies aimed at reducing poverty.

Analytic Strategy

We again use fuzzy-set techniques to analyze multiple advantages and multiple disadvantages. The central focus is on set coincidence, which is defined
as the degree to which two or more sets have overlapping memberships.
With two crisp sets, the calculation of set coincidence is simply the number
of cases that are in *both* sets (i.e., set intersection) divided by the number of
cases that are in *either* set (i.e., set union). With two fuzzy sets, the calculation is essentially the same, set intersection divided by set union; however,
the calculations of set intersection and set union take into account the fact
that set membership scores can take any value in the interval from 0 to 1.
The fuzzy-set calculations are as follows:

---

1. The calibration of the fuzzy sets that are based on these two variables are described in
chapter 4.

2. There is one very important exception to this generalization. As we show in this chapter,
black females who suffer multiple acute disadvantages consistently experience poverty.

$$\text{set intersection} = \Sigma \min(A_i, B_i)$$
$$\text{set union} = \Sigma \max(A_i, B_i)$$
$$\text{set coincidence} = \text{intersection/union,}$$

where "min" indicates the lower of the two values, "max" indicates the greater of the two values, and A_i and B_i are numerical membership scores in the two fuzzy sets, A and B. This formula extends directly to multiple fuzzy sets. With four fuzzy sets (A, B, C, and D), for example, the calculations are:

$$\text{set intersection} = \Sigma \min(A_i, B_i, C_i, D_i)$$
$$\text{set union} = \Sigma \max(A_i, B_i, C_i, D_i)$$
$$\text{set coincidence} = \text{intersection/union.}$$

These simple set-analytic principles can be extended to the calculation of the coincidence of any number of crisp or fuzzy sets. It is important to understand that the resulting set coincidence measures are primarily descriptive in nature. A set coincidence score of 1.0 indicates that the sets in question contain exactly the same cases, with identical membership scores; a score of 0 indicates that there are no overlapping memberships among the sets in question.

As we demonstrate in this chapter, set coincidence is not the same as correlation. Not only are their logics and metrics different, set coincidence is asymmetrical, while correlation is fully symmetrical. Table 6.1 illustrates this important contrast using hypothetical data. In this example, the researcher's goal is to assess the degree to which respondents combine medium-to-high parental income with medium-to-high test scores. Most respondents (500) combine the two advantages. A moderate number of respondents (200) have one advantage but not the other, and a small number have neither advantage (50). From a correlational viewpoint, the evidence is equivocal. In both columns of the table, cases are concentrated in the top cell, and the correlation is only .167, indicating a weak symmetrical connection between parental income and test scores. However, the calculation of set coincidence, focusing explicitly on the connection between medium-to-high parental income and medium-to-high test scores, indicates a very strong connection: 500/700 = .714, a 71.4% overlap. In other words, these two sets coincide substantially, a connection that is masked by the symmetric correlation coefficient.

The primary reason for the divergence of correlation and set coincidence is the fact that set coincidence is fundamentally asymmetrical. While the

Table 6.1 Coincidence versus correlation.

test scores	low parental income	medium–high parental income	Total
medium–high	100	500	600
low	50	100	150
total	150	600	750

Correlation = .167; coincidence of medium–high parental income with medium–high test scores = .714.

coincidence of moderate-to-high parental income and moderate-to-high test scores is very strong (.714), the connection between low parental income and low test scores is much weaker: 50/250 = .20, a 20% overlap. It follows from this example that the choice of sets matters a great deal when assessing set coincidence. This principle holds for the calculation of the coincidence of fuzzy sets as well.

Analysis of Multiple Advantages

In the analysis of multiple advantages that follows, we first calculate the set coincidence of *not-low-test-scores* with *not-low-income-parents*. We then include the fuzzy set of *educated* respondents in the mix and calculate the degree to which these three fuzzy sets coincide. Finally, we include degree of membership in the set of respondents with *educated-parents* and calculate the degree to which the four sets overlap. Our analysis of the coincidence of multiple disadvantages follows the same pattern, first showing the coincidence of two sets, then moving to the results for three and four sets.

Table 6.2 shows the degree to which advantages coincide. The analyses are computed separately for black females, black males, white females, and white males. For each sample, the first row shows the degree of set coincidence of *not-low-test-scores* and *not-low-income-parents*, the two sets that speak directly to the core of the *Bell Curve* debate. These results parallel analyses presented in chapter 5 and again show very strong racial differences. The degree of set coincidence for whites is nearly .80, while for blacks it is much lower, in the .40 range. In short, white advantage is well fortified by overlapping memberships in these two sets.

The second row of each race/gender panel shows the impact of the inclusion of degree of membership in the set of *educated* respondents on the calculation of set coincidence (three-way coincidence). For blacks the reduction in degree of set coincidence is substantial, to around .30. For whites, the degree of set coincidence is also reduced, but the level of set coincidence is still quite high at over .60. Finally, the third row of each panel shows the impact of the inclusion of degree of membership in the set of respondents with *educated-parents*. Again, the degree of set coincidence declines for all four groups, as should be expected, but the level of four-way set coincidence for whites is still high and above .5. The score of .556 for white females, for example, indicates that well over half of the membership in the union of these four sets is "covered" by shared memberships in all four sets (i.e., the intersection of these four sets). In contrast, the corresponding score for black females is .234, or just below a quarter of the membership in the union of all four sets. The substantial degree of white advantage in combining these four assets is further evidenced by the fact that whites' four-way set coincidence scores are still considerably higher than blacks' two-way set coincidence scores. In general, as more attributes are compounded, the ratio of multiple set intersection to multiple set union should be reduced substantially. In this light, the four-way set coincidence scores observed for whites are very high.

Perhaps just as striking as the differences in absolute levels of set coincidence is the *percentage reduction* in the degree of set coincidence, comparing the two-way set coincidence scores to the three- and four-way coincidence scores. For whites, the percentage reduction in set coincidence moving from the first row in each panel to the second row is about 20%; for blacks, the reduction is more than 30%. Comparing coincidence scores in the first row

Table 6.2 Coinciding advantages by race and gender.

Sample/fuzzy sets	Set coincidence
Black females	
not-low-test-score, not-low-income-parents	.421
not-low-test-score, not-low-income-parents, educated	.292
not-low-test-score, not-low-income-parents, educated, educated-parents	.234
Black males	
not-low-test-score, not-low-income-parents	.418
not-low-test-score, not-low-income-parents, educated	.291
not-low-test-score, not-low-income-parents, educated, educated-parents	.236
White females	
not-low-test-score, not-low-income-parents	.792
not-low-test-score, not-low-income-parents, educated	.643
not-low-test-score, not-low-income-parents, educated, educated-parents	.556
White males	
not-low-test-score, not-low-income-parents	.788
not-low-test-score, not-low-income-parents, educated	.628
not-low-test-score, not-low-income-parents, educated, educated-parents	.545

in each panel with the scores in the third row, the racial divergence is even stronger. For whites, the degree of set coincidence declines only about 30% across the three rows; for blacks the comparable calculation shows a percentage reduction in degree of set coincidence of about 44%. These stark differences provide further support for our argument that whites enjoy substantial combined and compounded advantages over blacks.

Analysis of Multiple Disadvantages

Table 6.3 presents our analysis of overlapping disadvantages for the four race/gender groups. In these analyses the first row of each panel shows the set coincidence scores for *not-high-test-scores* and *not-high-parental-income*, reproducing results presented in chapter 5. The pattern is clear: Blacks combine these two disadvantages to a much greater degree than whites. The two-way set coincidence scores for blacks exceed .80, while those for whites are in the .44 range. The second row of each panel shows the set coincidence of three disadvantages: *not-high-test-scores*, *not-high-income-parents*, and *not-highly-educated*. The drop in set coincidence is substantial for all four groups. However, the level of three-way set coincidence remains high for blacks: .516 for black females and .539 for black males. The third row of each panel shows the four-way set coincidence scores following the inclusion of the fourth disadvantage, *not-highly-educated-parents*. The set coincidence scores drop slightly for each sample. Still, the four-way set coincidence scores remain substantially higher for blacks than they are for whites, with a score of .485 for black females and a score of .488 for black males, compared to .277 for white females and .276 for white males. In short, the initial pattern of racial divergence in coinciding disadvantages observed for two disadvantages is maintained as more disadvantages are compounded. The pattern of overlapping disadvantages is strong for blacks and weak for whites.

Note that the strength of the four-way coincidence of *disadvantages* for blacks is almost as strong as the strength of the four-way coincidence of *advantages* shown for whites in table 6.2. In other words, the degree to which blacks face compounded disadvantages is almost as great as the degree to which whites enjoy compounded advantages. Notice also that the four-way coincidence scores for black disadvantage in table 6.3 are higher than the two-way coincidence scores for white disadvantage in the same table. This finding parallels the pattern shown in table 6.2, which documents the compounding of white advantage. Regarding the percentage reduction in the degree of set coincidence in disadvantages, comparing the two-way set coincidence scores to the three- and four-way coincidence scores across

Table 6.3 Coinciding disadvantages by race and gender.

Sample/fuzzy sets	Set coincidence
Black females	
not-high-test-score, not-high-income-parents	.824
not-high-test-score, not-high-income-parents, not-highly-educated	.516
not-high-test-score, not-high-income-parents, not-highly-educated, not-highly-educated-parents	.485
Black males	
not-high-test-score, not-high-income-parents	.806
not-high-test-score, not-high-income-parents, not-highly-educated	.539
not-high-test-score, not-high-income-parents, not-highly-educated, not-highly-educated-parents	.488
White females	
not-high-test-score, not-high-income-parents	.444
not-high-test-score, not-high-income-parents, not-highly-educated	.314
not-high-test-score, not-high-income-parents, not-highly-educated, not-highly-educated-parents	.277
White males	
not-high-test-score, not-high-income-parents	.438
not-high-test-score, not-high-income-parents, not-highly-educated	.322
not-high-test-score, not-high-income-parents, not-highly-educated, not-highly-educated-parents	.276

the four subgroups shows a greater similarity this time; for whites, the degree of set coincidence declines about 37% across the three rows while for blacks the percentage reduction is about 40%. In other words, as disadvantages are added, there appears to be less of a difference between whites and blacks compared to when advantages are added, suggesting again that there is asymmetry between the ways in which advantages and disadvantages combine.

The Contrast between Set Coincidence and Correlation

We now explore in more detail the contrast between conventional correlational analyses such as those of Herrnstein and Murray and Fischer et al. and the set-theoretic analyses we conduct here. While it is useful to treat causal conditions as competing "independent" variables and calculate their net effects on an outcome, it is also important to examine the degree to which advantages versus disadvantages are entwined—how they combine and reinforce. The analysis of set coincidence speaks directly to this issue. The strong evidence of coinciding advantages for whites and coinciding disadvantages for blacks reinforces our argument that it is the divergent entwining of these conditions that constitutes their most striking feature. It is this compounding that explains their potency as causal conditions. When advantages are compounded, as they are for whites, the beneficial impact of each condition is amplified and enhanced. Just the same, when disadvantages are compounded—the pattern for blacks—the detrimental impact of each condition is amplified, causing even further harm. Conventional correlational methods have a strictly symmetrical logic that makes them largely insensitive to divergent patterns of set coincidence.

As we have emphasized, set coincidence is not the same as correlation. In fact, it is possible to have strong set coincidence despite relatively weak correlations, as shown in table 6.1 using hypothetical data. Table 6.4 illustrates the same divergence of correlation and set coincidence using the *Bell Curve* data. The first panel reports the Pearson correlation coefficients for the six possible bivariate pairings of four fuzzy membership scores, now used as conventional variables.[3] The second panel shows these same six pairings, but the calculations are the two-way set coincidence scores using fuzzy sets: *not-low-income-parents*, *educated-parents*, *educated*, and *not-low-test-scores*. The third panel shows the same six pairings again, this time reporting the two-way set coincidence scores for the *negations* of the four fuzzy sets used in the second panel: *low-income-parents*, *not-educated-parents*, *not-educated*, and *low-test-scores*. These negations constitute what we call *acute* disadvantages. Observe that the same exact set of data is used in all three panels. The key difference is that the first panel shows the symmetric correlations, while the other two panels show asymmetric set coincidence scores. The only difference between the second and third panels is the fact that the membership scores used in the third panel are the negations of the membership scores used in the second panel; that is, the fuzzy membership scores have been reversed by subtracting each score from 1.0.[4]

The first panel of table 6.4 shows remarkable uniformity across race and gender in the degree to which these different attributes are correlated with each other. The correlations are moderate, ranging from .215 to .533, and

3. Very similar correlations result when the source (i.e., uncalibrated) variables are used in place of the fuzzy membership scores in the first panel.

4. The correlations among the negated fuzzy membership scores used in the third panel are the same as the correlations among the fuzzy membership scores used in the second panel and are reported in the first panel of the table.

Table 6.4 Bivariate correlations compared to set coincidence scores.

Panel 1

Correlations of fuzzy membership scores	Black females	Black males	White females	White males
parental income X parental education	.384	.358	.323	.348
parental income X respondent education	.322	.215	.247	.316
parental income X test score	.344	.293	.239	.313
parental education X respondent education	.387	.283	.501	.478
parental education X test score	.321	.329	.339	.373
respondent education X test score	.533	.490	.477	.518
average correlation by race/gender	.382	.328	.354	.391
average correlation by race	.355		.373	

Panel 2

Two-way coincidence of advantages	Black females	Black males	White females	White males
not low parental income X parent educated	.438	.463	.679	.681
not low parental income X respondent educated	.427	.441	.718	.708
not low parental income X not low test score	.421	.418	.792	.788
parent educated X respondent educated	.620	.623	.775	.767
parent educated X not low test score	.451	.457	.670	.672
respondent educated X no low test score	.538	.523	.745	.727
average set coincidence by race/gender	.483	.488	.730	.724
average set coincidence by race	.486		.727	

Panel 3

Two-way coincidence of acute disadvantages	Black females	Black males	White females	White males
low parental income X not educated parents	.565	.540	.295	.299
low parental income X not educated	.411	.420	.275	.292
low parental income X low test score	.555	.520	.195	.234
not educated parents X not educated	.538	.550	.563	.563
not educated parents X low test score	.506	.493	.216	.243
not educated X low test score	.450	.460	.259	.286
average set coincidence by race/gender	.504	.497	.301	.320
average set coincidence by race	.501		.311	

the average correlations for each race/gender group, shown in the next to last row of the first panel, are all about the same, ranging from .328 for black males to .391 for white males. Notice also that the strongest correlations (for example, the correlation between respondent education and test scores) tend to be strong across all four samples. The same is true for the weakest correlations (for example, the correlation between parental income and respondent education). In short, the correlational analysis offers a picture of race/gender uniformity and homogeneity, suggesting in turn that these causal conditions operate in the roughly same manner across race and gender.

The second and third panels of the table tell a very different story. In the second panel, which shows two-way coincidence scores for pairs of advantages, there is a very striking racial difference. Most of the set coincidence scores for white females and white males are in the .70 range, while most of the scores for black females and black males are in the .45 to .50 range. In fact, the average set coincidence of pairs of advantages is .727 for whites and .486 for blacks, indicating that paired advantages are much more common among whites than blacks. These results offer further support for our argument that whites enjoy a much higher level of reinforcing advantages—a pattern not shown by the correlational analysis.

Striking results are also revealed in the third panel, which shows two-way set coincidence scores for pairs of *acute* disadvantages. Most of the two-way coincidence scores for blacks are in the .45 to .55 range, with an average set coincidence of .501, while whites have much lower coincidence scores, mostly in the .20 to .32 range, with an average coincidence of .311. In fact, the average set coincidence scores for whites drops considerably, to .259, when the outlying set coincidence scores (for *not-educated-parent* coincidence with *not-educated* respondent) are omitted from the calculation of each average. These results indicate clearly that blacks experience a much higher level of combined acute disadvantages than whites, a pattern that is again not evident in the correlational analysis shown in the first panel.

Comparing the second and third panels to the first provides an interesting contrast. It appears that the correlational uniformity and race/gender homogeneity shown in the first panel may be due to divergent racial patterns in set coincidence scores that offset each other in the computation of the correlations. The set coincidence analysis shows that blacks have moderate levels of combined advantages and moderate levels of combined acute disadvantages. Whites, by contrast, have very high levels of combined advantages and low levels of combined acute disadvantages. Correlation, because of its symmetric nature, combines these racially divergent patterns into a single coefficient, washing out important differences and yielding, in the end, racially homogeneous results that obscure underlying racial heterogeneity in advantages and disadvantages.

While the general pattern of racial divergence is clear, it is important to point out that the underlying logic and metric of the calculation of set coincidence are very different from the logic and metric of the calculation of correlation. Their contrasting calculations speak to very different substantive questions. Our goal is not to argue that correlation is wrong and set coincidence is correct, or even to argue that one is better than the other. Rather, our goal is simply to observe that set coincidence provides different and useful descriptive evidence that cannot be gained using conventional correlational methods.

Multiple Advantages and the Avoidance of Poverty

We now turn our attention to the relationship between advantages and our first outcome of interest: the avoidance of poverty. Table 6.5 shows the set-analytic connection between multiple advantages and poverty avoidance. The first column shows different combinations of advantages, following the pattern of table 6.2. The second column (labeled "subset consistency") shows the consistency of the shared-outcome connection between membership in the set intersection listed in the first column and the avoidance of poverty. In other words, the calculations in the second column answer the question: how consistently do the people who combine the advantages listed in the first column avoid poverty?

The third column ("outcome coverage") shows the prevalence of the combination of advantages listed in the first column among those who avoid poverty. If the subset consistency calculation (second column) indicates that the cases with the combination of advantages listed in the first column constitute a consistent subset of instances of the outcome, then the outcome coverage column shows the degree to which respondents with the outcome display the combination of advantages shown in the first column— that is, to what degree respondents experiencing the outcome are accounted for or "covered" by this combination of advantage. When a combination of conditions constitutes a more-or-less consistent subset of the outcome (i.e., a very high score in the second column), the third column assesses the empirical relevance of the combination relative to all instances of the outcome (see also chapter 5).

In general, the supposition is that the combinations of sets listed in the first column should constitute consistent subsets of the outcome, with subset consistency scores greater than .75 and as close to 1.0 as possible. Furthermore, the expectation is that the consistency of the connection of combined advantages to avoiding poverty should increase as more advantages are added to the mix. In other words, as the number of combined advantages increases, the respondent's insulation from poverty should also increase. At the same time, as more advantages are compounded, the proportion of respondents with strong membership in the combination should

Table 6.5 The connection between multiple advantages and avoiding poverty.

Sample/fuzzy sets	Subset consistency	Outcome coverage
Black females		
not-low-test-scores, not-low-income-parents	0.791	0.416
not-low-test-scores, not-low-income-parents, educated	0.815	0.391
not-low-test-scores, not-low-income-parents, educated, educated-parents	0.823	0.326
Black males		
not-low-test-scores, not-low-income-parents	0.842	0.358
not-low-test-scores, not-low-income-parents, educated	0.866	0.322
not-low-test-scores, not-low-income-parents, educated, educated-parents	0.871	0.272
White females		
not-low-test-scores, not-low-income-parents	0.833	0.828
not-low-test-scores, not-low-income-parents, educated	0.876	0.713
not-low-test-scores, not-low-income-parents, educated, educated-parents	0.885	0.625
White males		
not-low-test-scores, not-low-income-parents	0.863	0.803
not-low-test-scores, not-low-income-parents, educated	0.900	0.675
not-low-test-scores, not-low-income-parents, educated, educated-parents	0.905	0.594

decrease. Accordingly, the prevalence of the combination among those who avoid poverty should also decrease, because fewer respondents display more elaborate combinations of advantages. The trade-off between the consistency of the subset relation (second column) and its outcome coverage (third column) is inherent in analyses of this type: greater refinement yields greater consistency at the price of smaller subsets and thus reduced coverage of the set of cases displaying the outcome.

Overall, the subset consistency scores reported in the middle column of table 6.5 are very good. They range from .791 (black females, two advantages) to .905 (white males, four advantages). For each sample, the consistency of the connection to avoiding poverty increases as the number of combined advantages increases. While the consistency scores are on average slightly lower for blacks than for whites and for females than for males, the main result is the finding that the consistency scores are relatively similar and strong across the board. These findings support the argument that the key to avoiding poverty is to combine advantages. Further, combining advantages works almost as well for blacks as it does for whites, as shown in the uniformly strong subset consistency scores across the four samples. The compounding of additional advantages, beyond the four used here, would likely result in a further convergence of the consistency scores at a very high level.

The important racial difference in table 6.5 is revealed in the last column, which addresses the prevalence of combined advantages among those who are not in poverty. As expected, outcome coverage declines for each sample as more advantages are compounded. For whites, however, the coverage scores are all very high, ranging from about .80 (two advantages) to about .60 (four advantages). In contrast, the scores for blacks are much lower, ranging from about .41 (two advantages) to .27 (four advantages). In other words, the outcome coverage scores for blacks, overall, are only about half the size of the scores for whites.

These findings have another implication, namely that there are blacks who are able avoid poverty despite the fact that they do not combine these specific advantages. To understand these results, it is important to take into account the much higher level of combined advantages in the white sample as a whole. The mean membership of the white males in the four-advantage combination (*not-low-test-scores, not-low-income-parents, educated,* and *educated-parents*) is .521; the corresponding figure for white females is even higher, .536. These statistics dwarf the figures for blacks: .183 for black females and .188 for black males. It appears that the lower prevalence of black respondents with combined advantages among those who avoid poverty reflects on the one hand the simple fact that blacks in general do not experience the very high level of combined advantages that whites enjoy and on the other the presence of other paths to avoiding poverty for blacks.

In table 6.6 we examine the set-analytic connections between combinations of *exceptional* advantages and avoiding poverty. This analysis offers an important contrast with table 6.5, which focuses on combinations of advantages that are at least moderate (see chapter 4). To operationalize exceptional advantages we utilize fuzzy sets with stricter thresholds. Specifically, instead of using "*not-low-income-parents,*" we substitute "*high-income-parents*"; for "*not-low-test-scores,*" we substitute "*high-test-scores*"; for "*educated,*" we substitute "*highly-educated*"; and for "*educated-parents,*" we substitute "*highly-educated-parents.*" Using stricter criteria provides a robustness check for table 6.5 and also provides an illustration of the trade-off between the exclusiveness of the conditions in a set-analytic formulation and the prevalence of these conditions among the cases displaying the outcome.

The middle column of table 6.6 reveals that there is a very strong and consistent connection between exceptional advantages and avoiding poverty.

Table 6.6 The connection between exceptional advantages and avoiding poverty.

Sample/fuzzy sets	Subset consistency	Outcome coverage
Black females		
high-test-scores, high-income-parents	.951	.029
high-test-scores, high-income-parents, highly-educated	.950	.028
high-test-scores, high-income-parents, highly-educated, highly-educated-parents	.946	.026
Black males		
high-test-scores, high-income-parents	.987	.034
high-test-scores, high-income-parents, highly-educated	.987	.033
high-test-scores, high-income-parents, highly-educated, highly-educated-parents	.986	.031
White females		
high-test-scores, high-income-parents	.928	.203
high-test-scores, high-income-parents, highly-educated	.941	.189
high-test-scores, high-income-parents, highly-educated, highly-educated-parents	.939	.166
White males		
high-test-scores, high-income-parents	.963	.229
high-test-scores, high-income-parents, highly-educated	.968	.213
high-test-scores, high-income-parents, highly-educated, highly-educated-parents	.965	.180

The subset consistency scores are all well above .90, with some close to 1.0. These results indicate that respondents with these characteristics consistently avoid poverty and that the connection between exceptional advantages and avoiding poverty holds regardless of race or gender. The striking differences in table 6.6 are in the outcome coverage column, which shows that only a tiny proportion of blacks—about 3%—who are not in poverty possess these combinations of exceptional advantages. These low prevalence numbers reflect the very low proportion of respondents in the black sample as a whole who combine these exceptional advantages. Whites, by contrast, have outcome coverage scores in the 20% range, which reflects the substantially greater prevalence of exceptional advantages in the white sample.

Overall, table 6.6 provides further evidence of the combinatorial nature of advantages and of the centrality of race to inequality in American society. The results also demonstrate that the more selective the criteria (i.e., the use of combinations of *exceptional* advantages), the greater the subset consistency scores across both race and gender. This high level of consistency, however, carries with it the cost of lower coverage.

Multiple Disadvantages and Poverty

Table 6.7 shows the results of the analysis of the connection between multiple disadvantages and poverty. The table format follows the pattern of table 6.5: the first column lists the relevant combinations of disadvantages; the second column shows the degree to which cases with each combination consistently share the outcome, poverty; and the third column reports the prevalence of the combination of conditions among the cases displaying the outcome. Again, the supposition is that respondents with combined disadvantages should constitute subsets of those in poverty (yielding high scores in the subset consistency column), and that compounding disadvantages should yield higher consistency scores.

While it is clear that the subset consistency scores in each of the four panels increase modestly as more disadvantages are compounded, overall the subset consistency scores are low. As might be expected, these scores are higher for blacks than for whites, with the scores for black females approaching the threshold of equivocal consistency. Black females who combine all four disadvantages have a consistency of .751 with the outcome *in-poverty*. Still, the broad pattern is one of inconsistency, and almost all the set-analytic connections examined in the middle column are well below the threshold of .75 consistency and thus too inconsistent to merit discussion.

The outcome coverage column, by contrast, reveals two strong connections. For both black females and black males, it is clear that *not-high-test-scores* and *not-high-income-parents* are widely shared antecedent conditions for poverty. A high outcome coverage score coupled with a modest subset consistency score indicates that the outcome (*in-poverty*) is a consistent subset of the causal combination of *not-high-test-scores* with *not-high-income-parents*. However, this connection, which duplicates findings presented in chapter 5, does not hold as more disadvantages are compounded with the first two, as evidenced by the declining coverage scores that suggest the outcome is no longer a consistent subset of the compounded disadvantage.[5]

The most noteworthy finding in table 6.7 is the modest connection between combined disadvantages and poverty for black females. Black females with *not-high-test-scores*, *not-high-income-parents*, *not-highly-educated*, and *not-highly-educated-parents* display a .751 subset consistency score. This modest connection warrants further examination, given that politicians

---

5. In other words, as the cumulative number of disadvantages increases from two to four, the consistency of the path towards the outcome increases, while simultaneously the coverage of the path decreases as fewer individuals share four than two disadvantages.

Table 6.7 The connection between multiple disadvantages and poverty.

Sample/fuzzy sets	Subset consistency	Outcome coverage
Black females		
not-high-test-scores, not-high-income-parents	0.606	0.920
not-high-test-scores, not-high-income-parents, not-highly-educated	0.743	0.706
not-high-test-scores, not-high-income-parents, not-highly-educated, not-highly-educated-parents	0.751	0.671
Black males		
not-high-test-scores, not-high-income-parents	0.461	0.917
not-high-test-scores, not-high-income-parents, not-highly-educated	0.557	0.742
not-high-test-scores, not-high-income-parents, not-highly-educated, not-highly-educated-parents	0.557	0.671
White females		
not-high-test-scores, not-high-income-parents	0.402	0.619
not-high-test-scores, not-high-income-parents, not-highly-educated	0.483	0.533
not-high-test-scores, not-high-income-parents, not-highly-educated, not-highly-educated-parents	0.490	0.488
White males		
not-high-test-scores, not-high-income-parents	0.371	0.640
not-high-test-scores, not-high-income-parents, not-highly-educated	0.425	0.550
not-high-test-scores, not-high-income-parents, not-highly-educated, not-highly-educated-parents	0.433	0.495

and policymakers alike along with the research community have noted the serious obstacles faced by black females. To address these political interests and policy concerns, we augment table 6.7 with an analysis of the set-analytic connections between the compounding of *acute* disadvantages and poverty. To operationalize acute disadvantages we utilize fuzzy sets with stricter thresholds. Specifically, for "*not-high-income-parents*," we substitute "*low-income-parents*"; for "*not-high-test-scores*," we substitute "*low-test-scores*"; for "*not-highly-educated*," we substitute "*not-educated*"; and for "*not-highly-educated-parents*," we substitute "*not-educated-parents*."[6]

In table 6.8 we present the results of our analysis of the connection between combinations of acute disadvantages and poverty. The pattern is clear: there is a strong connection between the compounding of acute disadvantages and poverty for black females but not for the three other race/

6. We describe the calibration of these fuzzy sets in chapter 4.

Table 6.8 The connection between acute disadvantages and poverty.

Sample/fuzzy sets	Subset consistency	Outcome coverage
Blacks females		
low-test-scores, low-income-parents	0.791	0.619
low-test-scores, low-income-parents, not-educated	0.857	0.378
low-test-scores, low-income-parents, not-educated, not-educated-parents	0.861	0.346
Blacks males		
low-test-scores, low-income-parents	0.553	0.539
low-test-scores, low-income-parents, not-educated	0.644	0.371
low-test-scores, low-income-parents, not-educated, not-educated-parents	0.646	0.329
White females		
low-test-scores, low-income-parents	0.677	0.134
low-test-scores, low-income-parents, not-educated	0.690	0.111
low-test-scores, low-income-parents, not-educated, not-educated-parents	0.681	0.098
White males		
low-test-scores, low-income-parents	0.627	0.190
low-test-scores, low-income-parents, not-educated	0.673	0.171
low-test-scores, low-income-parents, not-educated, not-educated-parents	0.679	0.148

gender samples. The subset consistency column shows that black females with different combinations of acute disadvantages share poverty as an outcome and that this connection increases in consistency as additional disadvantages are compounded. The subset consistency scores for the other three race/gender groups are too low to warrant attention. Note also that the connection between acute disadvantages and poverty for black females is again not revealed in a correlational analysis. Thus, while the general pattern is one of inconsistent connections between combinations of disadvantages and poverty, the results for black females provide a conspicuous exception, especially when the focus is on combinations of acute disadvantages. Based on these results, it is clear that policymakers should make a concerted effort to address the obstacles faced by black females in poverty.

Multiple Disadvantages and Being "At Risk" for Poverty

In order to maintain direct relevance to the *Bell Curve* debate, the analyses presented in this chapter focus on two outcomes: degree of membership in the set of cases in poverty and degree of membership in the set of cases avoiding poverty. We show that the causal conditions that are commonly used in quantitative analyses of poverty are strongly linked to the outcome *not-in-poverty*, while the connections to *in-poverty* are much less consistent. We have also shown very strong evidence of racial differences, especially white advantage, when it comes to combining advantages and linking these advantages to the avoidance of poverty. These results reflect our explicit focus on *in-poverty* and *not-in-poverty* as outcomes. However, as previous research has shown (e.g., Duncan and Rodgers, 1988; Duncan et al., 1995), being in poverty is not necessarily a persistent condition marked by an unchanging underclass but is frequently a transitional state, with low-income individuals hovering at the brink of poverty or being able to exit poverty after a relatively brief stint below the poverty line, perhaps only to reenter poverty. Accordingly, a measure that identifies those at risk of poverty is of considerable relevance to antipoverty measures (e.g., Neff, 2013). To better reflect this pattern, in this section we shift the focus to degree of membership in the set of respondents who are "low income." The set of low-income respondents is more inclusive than the set of respondents in poverty; it includes not only those who are in poverty, but also those who are at risk of being in poverty because of their relatively close proximity to the poverty line. Using the set of respondents potentially at risk of experiencing poverty is also instructive because it provides additional insight into the spectrum of policy decisions relevant to averting poverty.

To calibrate degree of membership in *low-income*, we use the same source variable we used for calibrating *in-poverty*—the ratio of household income to the poverty level for that household size and composition. However, we calibrate this ratio so that the resulting set is more inclusive than the *in-poverty* set. Recall that respondents with incomes at or below the poverty level (ratio of household income to poverty level ≤ 1.0) achieve full membership in the *in-poverty* set. By contrast, full membership in the set of respondents with *low-income* is now achieved by respondents whose income is double the poverty level (ratio of household income to poverty level ≤ 2.0). Thus, many more respondents have substantial membership in the *low-income* set than in the *in-poverty* set because more respondent have income-to-poverty ratios that are ≤ 2.0 than have income-to-poverty ratios that are ≤ 1.0.[7]

Table 6.9 reports the results of the analysis of the set-analytic connections between combinations of disadvantages and low-income. The table follows the same format as table 6.7; the only difference is the calibration

7. The cross-over point (.50) for degree of membership in low-income is an income-to-poverty ratio of 3.0; the threshold for nonmembership (.05) is an income-to-poverty ratio of 5.5.

Table 6.9 The connection between multiple disadvantages and being at risk for poverty.

Sample/fuzzy sets	Subset consistency	Outcome coverage
Black females		
not-high-test-scores, not-high-income-parents	0.812	0.880
not-high-test-scores, not-high-income-parents, not-highly-educated	0.908	0.616
not-high-test-scores, not-high-income-parents, not-highly-educated, not-highly-educated-parents	0.912	0.582
Black males		
not-high-test-scores, not-high-income-parents	0.715	0.881
not-high-test-scores, not-high-income-parents, not-highly-educated	0.801	0.661
not-high-test-scores, not-high-income-parents, not-highly-educated, not-highly-educated-parents	0.807	0.603
White females		
not-high-test-scores, not-high-income-parents	0.692	0.529
not-high-test-scores, not-high-income-parents, not-highly-educated	0.775	0.426
not-high-test-scores, not-high-income-parents, not-highly-educated, not-highly-educated-parents	0.780	0.387
White males		
not-high-test-scores, not-high-income-parents	0.666	0.534
not-high-test-scores, not-high-income-parents, not-highly-educated	0.733	0.441
not-high-test-scores, not-high-income-parents, not-highly-educated, not-highly-educated-parents	0.742	0.394

of the outcome. The general pattern is one of much stronger set-analytic connections. The subset consistency scores for black females are all very strong, ranging from .812 (two disadvantages) to .912 (four disadvantages). The outcome coverage scores for black females are also substantial, indicating that many black females who are low-income share these disadvantages. The results for black males mirror the results for black females, but are weaker. The black male results for three-way and four-way combinations of disadvantages both exceed the .80 consistency threshold, but these scores are still a full ten points below the corresponding figures for black females. The results for white females remain equivocal, with subset consistency scores for three-way and four-way disadvantages between .75 and .80. Finally, the subset consistency scores for white males do not reach even the equivocal threshold (.75). In essence, the pattern across the four race/gender groups closely mirrors the status hierarchy of American society. There is a very strong racial difference, favoring whites, coupled with a modest gender difference within each racial group, favoring males. The lower the status of the race/gender group, the more consistent the shared-outcome connection between combined disadvantages and low-income.

More generally, these results serve as an additional robustness check on our core analyses (shown in tables 6.5 through 6.8) and provide further evidence in support of the broad portrait of inequality we present. Substantively, the findings indicate that the set-analytic connection between combined disadvantages and being at risk for poverty is stronger than the set-analytic connection between combined disadvantages and being in poverty.

Conclusion

The main conclusion we draw from our set coincidence analysis of advantages and disadvantages is that whites more than blacks experience overlapping and reinforcing advantages, while blacks more than whites experience overlapping and reinforcing disadvantages. Furthermore, the prevalence of combined advantages among those who avoid poverty is much higher for whites than for blacks. Thus, our main findings center on the unambiguous racial divide evident in virtually all of our analyses. The major exception to this generalization is the connection between multiple acute disadvantages and experiencing poverty. How consistently do respondents with multiple acute disadvantages experience poverty as an outcome? Our results indicate a highly consistent connection for black females, but not for the other three race/gender samples.

It is important to emphasize that the comparison of tables 6.5 and 6.7 makes it clear that the causal conditions that researchers and policy makers alike favor in conventional quantitative analyses of poverty are most useful when it comes to accounting for the avoidance of poverty; they are not as potent when it comes to explaining how people succumb to poverty. The asymmetric nature of how causes combine and connect to the absence versus the presence of an outcome speaks to a fundamental issue of causal accumulation. Specifically, our findings provide support for a pattern of causal accumulation that is dependent on what we refer to as the *intentionality* of the outcome—the degree to which an outcome is something that the actors involved strive to achieve (e.g., avoiding poverty) versus an outcome that is not intended (e.g., falling into poverty). As our results indicate, outcome intentionality—either through the direct agency of the actors or through institutionalized support structures—appears to result in more consistent patterns of causal accumulation when intentionality is present, and in much less consistent patterns when intentionality is absent. We will return to this issue in the final chapter where we discuss the implications of our results for policy makers.

SEVEN

Intersectional Analysis of Causal Conditions Linked to Avoiding Poverty

In chapter 6 we examined four main set-analytic connections: the links between (1) combinations of advantages and avoiding poverty, (2) combinations of *exceptional* advantages and avoiding poverty, (3) combinations of disadvantages and experiencing poverty, and (4) combinations of *acute* disadvantages and experiencing poverty. Considering both set-analytic criteria—subset consistency and outcome coverage—the first link, between combinations of advantages and avoiding poverty, is by far the strongest. This chapter explores this important connection in greater depth.

The analysis presented in this chapter offers a distinctly different approach to the evidence examined in chapters 5 and 6. Those two chapters both focused on race/gender contrasts in the coincidence and impact of combinations of advantages versus disadvantages. The different combinations were specified in advance and not derived independently for each sample. In contrast, we now turn our focus to the examination of *compositional differences* across the four race/gender samples in "causal recipes" linked to avoiding poverty. Using set-analytic methods, it is possible to derive causal recipes showing the combinations of advantages consistently linked to avoiding poverty for each race/gender sample. For instance, are there consistent compositional differences between the recipes for whites versus blacks or between those for males versus females? How do the causal recipes for the four groups compare with respect to the role of education or the role of family background? Compositional differences in causal recipes across the four race/gender samples provide important information about the structure and dynamics of social inequality.

The examination of compositional differences in causal recipes is *not* the same as assessing the relative importance of causal variables, which is the central preoccupation of conventional quantitative analysts. Often, social

scientists want to know: *"Under what conditions* is there a connection between a specific causal condition and an outcome?" Another way to think
about this issue is in terms of enabling contexts: *In what contexts* is there a
link between a specific causal condition and the outcome? Consider a simple hypothetical example. Suppose the analysis reveals that having good test
scores, by itself, is linked to avoiding poverty for white males, but for black
males good test scores must be combined with being well educated in order
to avoid poverty—that is, both must be present for this outcome to occur.
In effect, these results would indicate that having good test scores would
"work" for black males only when combined with institutional validation
(e.g., a diploma), whereas this type of validation would not be required for
white males.

This focus on causal recipes and enabling contexts contrasts sharply with
the focus of conventional quantitative analysis. The causal recipes question is
directed toward identifying the different combinations of conditions consistently linked to an outcome, which in turn allows specification of the contexts
in which there is an empirical link between a given causal condition and the
outcome. Conventional quantitative analysis, by contrast, typically focuses on
the question, "What is the net effect of X on Y, adjusting for the confounding
effects of causal variables that are correlated with X?" Both questions are important. The first is focused on causal combinations and contexts; the second
is directed toward isolating the average importance of X as a cause of Y across
a range of diverse contexts (i.e., X's average treatment effect). It is possible for
X's net effect in a conventional analysis to be nil or even negative, despite its
role as a contributing cause in specific contexts. It is also possible for X's net
effect to be statistically significant, while the context in which this connection
exists may be relatively circumscribed (though also relatively common). The
important point is that these two questions, about causal recipes and contexts
versus net effects, address different causal questions.[1]

Consider the policy implications of the answers to the two types of
questions posed above. The contexts question is relevant to the problem
of making decisive interventions. Answers to this question provide useful
information about relevant contexts and are action oriented. Under what
conditions will a specific intervention (X) have its desired impact (Y)? The

1. Note that the use of interaction effects in conventional quantitative analysis does not
provide the same kind of insight as the assessment of recipes and enabling contexts. While
interaction terms and causal recipes appear to be similar, the use of interaction terms mainly
provides a test for the significance of nonadditive effects. In contrast, the set-theoretic analysis
of causal recipes provides a direct assessment of the different, and often complex, combinations
of conditions that are strongly and consistently linked to an outcome (e.g., avoiding poverty).

net effects question is relevant to the problem of assessing an intervention's *average* impact across a range of diverse contexts. For example, if X is increased across-the-board, will the general impact on Y be positive, neutral, or negative, considering all cases? Again, both questions are important, and they are distinct—the answer to one question does not imply or entail the answer to the other.

Because it is set-analytic in nature, truth table analysis, a procedure implemented in QCA (Qualitative Comparative Analysis), is especially well-suited for answering the contexts question; it is not an appropriate tool for the net effects question. The usual QCA result is a set of causal recipes specifying the different intersections of conditions that are consistently linked to a given outcome, which in turn circumscribe subsets of cases that consistently display the outcome. These recipes can be evaluated to see which ones involve a condition of interest, thereby allowing the researcher to specify the contexts—the relevant additional conditions that must be present—that enable a connection between that condition and the outcome.

To answer these and related questions we derive causal recipes for each race/gender sample using truth table techniques elaborated by Ragin (1987, 2000, 2008). We begin with a detailed explanation of the analysis of the causal recipes linked to staying out of poverty for white males and then present the results of the corresponding analyses for the other three race/gender samples.

The Intersectional Logic of Truth Table Analysis

Intersectional analysis views cases as *combinations* of aspects. Using an intersectional approach to the NLSY data, for example, a researcher would focus on different *combinations* of race, gender, family background, respondent's education, respondent's test scores, and so on. Intersectional theory, which inspires this focus on combinations, holds that individuals should be viewed holistically, in terms of the characteristics or aspects that are brought together in each case. For example, a black, low-income, well-educated female should be viewed as a specific combination of attributes and not pigeonholed according to any single overriding trait (e.g., as "black" or as "female"). Note that one of the underlying principles of intersectionality theory, which we implement using truth table analysis, is that a single difference between two otherwise identical configurations of characteristics (e.g., a difference in family background) may constitute a qualitative difference between the two configurations. In other words, two individuals may be worlds apart even though they differ by only one among many important aspects.

Truth table analysis (Ragin, 1987, 2000, 2008) provides a means for addressing combinations of characteristics. The truth table approach is fully intersectional in nature and thus directly implements the core insight of intersectionality theory. The rows of a truth table are formed from the logically possible combinations of causally relevant conditions or attributes. Each condition is considered in a bivalent manner, as either present or absent, or when using fuzzy sets, in terms of its *degree* of presence or absence.[2] Consider a truth table constructed from four fuzzy-set causal conditions: *educated/ not-educated, not-low-test-scores/low-test-scores, favorable-family-background/ unfavorable-family-background,* and *favorable-domestic-situation/unfavorable-domestic-situation.*[3] This truth table has sixteen rows, ranging in ascending binary order from all four disadvantages (row #1: *not-educated, low-test-scores, unfavorable-family-background,* and *unfavorable-domestic-situation*) to all four advantages (row #16: *educated, not-low-test-scores, favorable-family-background,* and *favorable-domestic-situation*), as shown in table 7.1. From an intersectional perspective, each row of this truth table represents a different kind of case. Thus, table 7.1 displays sixteen different kinds of cases.

Each row of the truth table includes a count of the number of conforming cases. Each case (i.e., each survey respondent) has a degree of membership in each of the four sets that define the rows of the truth table. The degree to which each case is a member of each row can be calculated using fuzzy algebra. Suppose, for example, a case has a membership score of .6 in *"educated,"* a score of .7 in *"not-low-test-scores,"* a score of .8 in *"favorable-family-background,"* and a score of .6 in *"favorable-domestic-situation."* This person's membership in row #16 (the combination of these four advantages) is equal to:

min (.6, .7, .8, .6) = .6

This case is more in than out of the set represented by the last row because its membership score is greater than .5, the cross-over point. Accordingly, this case is included in the count of cases for that row. As shown in Ragin (2008), a case can have a membership score greater than .5 in one and only one row of the truth table. This mathematical property provides the basis for the count of conforming cases shown in the penultimate column of table 7.1. The property holds true despite the fact that a case can have a nonzero degree of membership in every row of the truth table; however, that

2. "Absence" in this analytic context means "negated," as in married versus not-married. It does not indicate irrelevance. With fuzzy sets, negation is accomplished by subtracting membership scores from 1.0. For example, a case with a membership score of .8 in *"educated"* has a membership score of .2 in *"not-educated."*

3. The calibration of these four fuzzy sets is discussed in chapter 4.

Table 7.1 Truth table showing combinations of causal conditions linked to avoiding poverty: white male sample.

Row #	Educated	Not-low test scores	Favorable family background	Favorable domestic situation	Number of conforming cases	Subset consistency
1	no	no	no	no	25	.68
2	no	no	no	yes	43	.73
3*	no	no	yes	no	11	.80
4*	no	no	yes	yes	6	.83
5*	no	yes	no	no	6	.85
6*	no	yes	no	yes	11	.88
7*	no	yes	yes	no	16	.87
8*	no	yes	yes	yes	17	.90
9*	yes	no	no	no	14	.78
10	yes	no	no	yes	28	.81
11	yes	no	yes	no	31	.83
12	yes	no	yes	yes	34	.86
13	yes	yes	no	no	72	.87
14	yes	yes	no	yes	114	.90
15	yes	yes	yes	no	377	.89
16	yes	yes	yes	yes	550	.93

*Rows that fail to meet the frequency threshold of 1.5% of cases. Together these seven low-frequency rows embrace about 6% of the cases.

nonzero degree membership will always be less than .5. For example, this same case's degree of membership in the first row of the truth table (which is the complete opposite of the sixteenth row) is equal to:

$$\min (1-.6, 1-.7, 1-.8, 1-.6) = \min(.4, .3, .2, .4) = .2$$

The count of conforming cases, therefore, shows the number of cases with greater than .5 membership in a given combination of conditions. In other words, it is a count of the cases that are more in than out of the set defined by the intersection of the four fuzzy sets specified in each row. The four fuzzy sets also can be seen as constituting a four-dimensional vector space with sixteen sectors (a hypercube). In this view, the number of conforming cases reported for each row of table 7.1 is a count of the cases residing in each sector. As long as a case has no fuzzy membership scores equal to .5, it resides in a specific sector of the vector space.[4]

As table 7.1 reveals, the distribution of white males in the four-dimensional vector space defined by these four fuzzy-set causal conditions

4. Cases with exact membership scores of .5 cannot be assigned to one and only one sector of the vector space since they are equidistant from the corresponding corners of the hypercube. In truth table analysis, such cases are not counted in the "number of conforming cases" column.

is remarkably uneven. The sector with the most cases is #16, which embraces 550 individuals. More than 40% of white males reside in this single sector, where all four advantages intersect. The second most populated sector is the combination of educated, not-low test scores, favorable family background, and a *not*-favorable domestic situation. This configuration captures 28% of white males, which brings the cumulative percentage of cases to 68%. In other words about two-thirds of white males combine three key advantages—*educated, not-low-test-scores*, and *favorable-family-background*. The four most populated sectors (#13 through #16) together capture an impressive 82% of white males. These four sectors embrace white males combining two key advantages—*educated* and *not-low-test-scores*.

Table 7.1 further reveals that there are sectors that contain very few cases. In fact, seven of the sectors (#3 through #9) each contain less than 1.5% of the cases. Together, these seven sectors embrace only 6% of the cases. An important decision in an analysis of this type is the selection of a frequency threshold for the inclusion of row configurations in the truth table analysis. When a row frequency is low, there may not be sufficient empirical evidence to warrant assessing the degree to which membership in a causal combination (e.g., as specified in a truth table row) is a consistent subset of membership in the outcome. In other words, if a row has too few cases, there may not be enough evidence to permit the assignment of an outcome score to the row. When working with a large-N, individual-level data set, it is especially important to establish a substantial frequency threshold because (1) random measurement and assignment error are both likely to be non-trivial, and (2) researchers typically have little or no case-level knowledge to fall back on. While it is important to select a substantial frequency threshold when using data of this type, it is also important to capture the bulk of the cases in the sample. In other words, the concern for robustness argues in favor of a higher frequency cut-off, while the concern for inclusiveness and sample coverage argues in favor of a more moderate frequency cut-off. Based on a careful analysis of all four samples, we selected a row frequency threshold of 1.5% of cases. This frequency threshold captures 98% of black females (ten rows), 97% of black males (eleven rows), 95% of white females (nine rows), and 94% of white males (nine rows) and is thus sufficiently inclusive while also avoiding rows with too few cases for a robust assessment of the outcome.[5]

---

5. The frequency threshold for white males is 21; for white females, 20; for black males, 11; and for black females, 12.

The unevenness of the distribution of cases across the different combinations of set memberships is directly relevant to the concerns of intersectionality theory. It is not accidental, for example, that 40% of white males combine all four advantages or that there are very few white males who possess either *not-low-test-scores* or *educated* as their only advantage. Such irregularities in the distribution of cases across combinations have a profound impact on social perceptions and the tendency to infer additional attributes that may or may not be present.

Causal Recipes for Avoiding Poverty: White Males

To illustrate our analytic approach, we first present detailed truth table analyses for white males and then present the results for the other three samples in a more abbreviated format. When using truth tables to derive causal recipes, the researcher codes an outcome value for each row, based on the subset consistency score for that row. The subset consistency score shows the degree to which membership in the row can be considered a subset of membership in the outcome, which in turn can be interpreted as the degree to which the cases in a given row agree in expressing the outcome. A consistency score of 1.0 indicates that cases with a given combination of characteristics uniformly display the outcome. Scores of .85 or higher indicate very good levels of subset consistency.

Table 7.1 uses degree of membership in the set of respondents who successfully avoid poverty as the outcome condition. For each row of the truth table, there is a report of the assessment of the degree to which cases in that row constitute a consistent subset of the cases that are not in poverty (shown in the last column). Table 7.2 shows the coding of three outcomes, defined below, based on the consistency scores reported in table 7.1. In effect, table 7.2 summarizes the key connections between combinations of advantages/disadvantages and avoiding poverty for white males.

The logic of truth table analysis is easiest to grasp visually. For illustration, consider figure 7.1, which is a graphical representation of table 7.2. The figure shows the four intersecting sets and the sixteen different set intersections generated by these four sets. The sixteen set intersections in figure 7.2 are labeled according to their corresponding row numbers in table 7.2. Subset consistency is greyscale coded to show the degree of consistency for the truth table rows with subset consistency scores. The highest subset consistency scores ($\geq$ .90) are coded black; the next highest ($\geq$ .85 and < .90) are coded dark grey; and the third highest ($\geq$ .80 and < .85) are coded medium grey. These codings form the basis for the three nested outcomes shown

Table 7.2 Truth table for white males showing the three outcomes.

Row #	Educated	Not-low test scores	Favorable family background	Favorable domestic situation	Number of conforming cases	Cons. ≥ .90	Cons. ≥ .85	Cons. ≥ .80
1	no	no	no	no	25	0	0	0
2	no	no	no	yes	43	0	0	0
3*	no	no	yes	no	11	-	-	-
4*	no	no	yes	yes	6	-	-	-
5*	no	yes	no	no	6	-	-	-
6*	no	yes	no	yes	11	-	-	-
7*	no	yes	yes	no	16	-	-	-
8*	no	yes	yes	yes	17	-	-	-
9*	yes	no	no	no	14	-	-	-
10	yes	no	no	yes	28	0	0	1
11	yes	no	yes	no	31	0	0	1
12	yes	no	yes	yes	34	0	1	1
13	yes	yes	no	no	72	0	1	1
14	yes	yes	no	yes	114	1	1	1
15	yes	yes	yes	no	377	0	1	1
16	yes	yes	yes	yes	550	1	1	1

*Indicates rows that fail to meet the frequency threshold of 1.5% of cases.

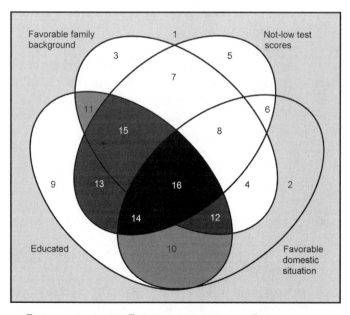

■ Subset consistency ≥ 0.90; ■ subset consistency 0.85 → 0.89; ■ subset consistency 0.80 → 0.84; ■ subset consistency < 0.80; [ ] below frequency threshold of 1.5% of cases.

7.1. Venn diagram showing causal recipes for avoiding poverty: white male sample.

in table 7.2: consistency ≥ .90; consistency ≥ .85, and consistency ≥ .80. There are two rows with consistency ≥ .90, five rows with consistency ≥ .85, and seven rows with consistency ≥ .80. Rows with subset consistency < .80 are coded light grey; rows that fail to meet the frequency threshold of 1.5% of the sample are left blank (white).

Truth table analysis proceeds by identifying pairs of rows that consistently share an outcome yet differ by only one characteristic. This single difference between a pair of such rows is irrelevant to the outcome in question, and the aspect that differs can be eliminated from the pair, yielding a single combined row. Application of this method of elimination continues until no further simplification is possible. Consider, for example, the two combinations coded black (row 14 and row 16 in table 7.2), indicating very high set-theoretic consistency (i.e., highly consistent poverty avoidance):[6]

> *educated•not-low-test-scores•favorable-family-background• favorable-domestic-situation + educated•not-low-test-scores• unfavorable-family-background•favorable-domestic-situation.*

It is clear from this pairing of cases that family background does not matter in the presence of *educated•not-low-test-scores•favorable-domestic-situation.* The consistency of the link to avoiding poverty is very high for both rows and thus also for their logical reduction into a single combination of three conditions:

> *educated•not-low-test-scores•favorable-domestic-situation.*

Turning to figure 7.1, it is clear that the two black sectors exactly fill the space where these three sets intersect.

Next, consider this same analysis using the five rows with subset consistency scores ≥ .85. First, notice that rows 13 through 16 all display the outcome. Further, the rows can be combined into simplified expressions. For instance, Rows 13 and 14 are identical except that one includes a favorable domestic situation while the other does not, so both rows can be combined to yield a simplified recipe:

> *educated•not-low-test-scores•unfavorable-family-background.*

In a similar manner, rows 15 and 16 can be combined to yield:

> *educated•not-low-test-scores•favorable-family-background.*

---

6. The "•" symbol indicates set intersection—logical *and*; the "+" symbol indicates set union—logical *or*.

These two three-condition configurations can be further combined to produce a two-condition causal recipe:

educated•not-low-test-scores.

The intersection of these two sets is plainly visible in figure 7.1, involving two black-coded sectors and two dark-grey-coded sectors (i.e., rows 13, 14, 15 and 16). Rows 12 and 16 also can be combined to yield a single three-condition recipe:

educated•favorable-family-background•favorable-domestic-situation.

This recipes demonstrates that it is possible for white males to avoid poverty at a high level of consistency ($\geq$ .85) while also having low test scores.

We present the results for consistency $\geq$ .80 without detailing the step-by-step reductions:

educated•not-low-test-scores +
educated•favorable-family-background +
educated•favorable-domestic-situation.

These three two-condition recipes can be factored to show the centrality of being educated to poverty avoidance for white males:[7]

educated•(not-low-test-scores + favorable-family-background +
favorable-domestic-situation).

In this formulation of the results, the three causal conditions in parentheses are substitutable, meaning that having any one of the three completes the recipe. The importance of being educated as a common causal condition is also visible in figure 7.1. All seven of the relevant intersections are contained within the confines of the educated set. The one blank intersection within the educated set (sector 9) is excluded because it does not meet the frequency threshold for truth table analysis (see table 7.1). Finally, note that with four causal conditions, there are six *logically possible* combinations of two advantages. For white males, three of these six combinations provide protection from poverty—the three that include being educated as one of the two advantages.

---

7. While it is tempting to interpret the common ingredient, *educated,* as a necessary condition, this interpretation requires the support of a separate test of the superset relationship. We note that *educated* does not pass this test and therefore should not be interpreted as a necessary condition (or as a shared antecedent condition). It is simply a common ingredient across the derived recipes.

Table 7.3 Truth table results for white males not-in-poverty.

Consistency threshold	Causal recipe	Subset consistency	Outcome coverage
.90	educated•not-low-test-scores•favorable-domestic-situation	.915	.552
.85	educated•not-low-test-scores + educated•	.886	.732
	favorable-family-background•favorable-domestic-situation	.921	.498
.80	educated•not-low-test-scores + educated•	.886	.732
	favorable-family-background + educated•	.900	.621
	favorable-domestic-situation	.906	.588

The centrality of education in the truth table results for poverty avoidance contrasts sharply with the focus of the *Bell Curve* debate on 'family background *versus* test scores.' In the set-analytic results for consistency ≥ .80, *not-low-test-scores* and *favorable-family-background* are substitutable conditions, as is having a *favorable-domestic-situation*. One of these three conditions must be combined with being educated in order to provide protection from poverty.

Table 7.3 reports the results of the truth table analyses specified in table 7.2, using the three nested outcomes. Table 7.3 reports not only the causal recipes, but also their separate subset consistency and outcome coverage scores. Notice that the recipes derived in the first analysis (consistency ≥ .90) constitute a subset of the recipes derived in the second analysis (consistency ≥ .85), which in turn constitute a subset of the recipes derived in the third analysis (consistency ≥ .80). These subset relations follow from the nesting of the three outcomes, as shown in table 7.2. The compositional differences across the recipes indicate how a recipe must be amended in order to reach a higher level of consistency. For example, in order to reach .90 consistency, a two-condition recipe consistent at the .85 level may have to be augmented with a third ingredient, thus narrowing and refining the set of cases covered by the recipe.

As noted in the opening paragraphs of this chapter, the results of a truth table analysis reveal the contexts or conditions that enable specific causal connections. For example, the results using a consistency threshold of .80 indicate that having *not-low-test-scores* offers protection from poverty only when it is combined with being educated. The same is true for the condition *favorable-family-background*—it offers protection from poverty only when combined with being *educated*. To reach the highest level of consistency (.90), *not-low-test-scores* must be combined with both being *educated* and having a *favorable-domestic-situation*. These results contrast sharply with both the *Bell Curve* and *Inequality by Design*, with their common focus on the net effects of these conditions.

Finally, it is important to note that the outcome coverage scores for white males are generally very high, ranging from .552 to .732. These calculations show the degree to which each causal recipe covers or accounts for the sum of the fuzzy membership scores in the outcome of avoiding poverty. It is also possible to calculate the joint coverage of two or more recipes. The joint coverage of the recipes derived using the .85 consistency threshold is .754, while joint coverage of the recipes derived using the .80 consistency threshold is .773. It is clear from these calculations that joint coverage is not much higher than the coverage of the individual recipes. This finding further underscores the overlapping nature of the causal recipes derived in these analyses, again pointing to their intersectional nature—in fact, 40% of white males combine all four advantages.

Causal Recipes for Avoiding Poverty: White Females

We turn now to the analysis of the causal recipes linking configurations of advantages/disadvantage to poverty avoidance for white females. Our starting point is table 7.4, which shows the truth table for white females, structured in the same fashion as table 7.2 for white males. Overall, the patterns for white females are very similar to those for white males. The same seven rows (3 through 9) fail to meet the frequency threshold of 1.5% of cases. Together, these seven rows embrace about 6% of the cases. Also, the most populated sector is again row #16, the combination of all four advantages. This sector captures 46% of white females. The only difference, albeit slight, between white females and white males is in the coding of two of the outcomes. While the coding of the outcome using consistency ≥ .90 is the same, females have one less row coded 1 for consistency ≥ .85 and also one less row coded 1 for consistency ≥ .80. Figure 7.2 offers a graphical representation of table 7.4. The three outcomes are grey-scale-coded in the same manner as in figure 7.1 Again, the most remarkable feature of the white female patterns is their similarity to white male patterns. The high consistency sectors are very similar, and they are all subsets of the set of *educated* respondents.

Table 7.5 presents the detailed results of the truth table analyses specified in table 7.4 and depicted in figure 7.2. As noted already, the white female results for consistency ≥ .90 are the same as the white male results. The subset consistency and outcome coverage scores, however, are slightly higher for white females. For consistency ≥ .85, the white female recipes are slightly

Table 7.4 Truth table for white females showing the three outcomes.

Row #	Educated	Not-low test scores	Favorable family background	Favorable domestic situation	Number of conforming cases	Cons. ≥ .90	Cons. ≥ .85	Cons. ≥ .80
1	no	no	no	no	20	0	0	0
2	no	no	no	yes	20	0	0	0
3*	no	no	yes	no	4	-	-	-
4*	no	no	yes	yes	8	-	-	-
5*	no	yes	no	no	7	-	-	-
6*	no	yes	no	yes	11	-	-	-
7*	no	yes	yes	no	8	-	-	-
8*	no	yes	yes	yes	16	-	-	-
9*	yes	no	no	no	16	-	-	-
10	yes	no	no	yes	33	0	0	1
11	yes	no	yes	no	23	0	0	0
12	yes	no	yes	yes	29	0	1	1
13	yes	yes	no	no	89	0	0	1
14	yes	yes	no	yes	130	1	1	1
15	yes	yes	yes	no	293	0	1	1
16	yes	yes	yes	yes	602	1	1	1

*Indicates rows that fail to meet the frequency threshold of 1.5% of cases.

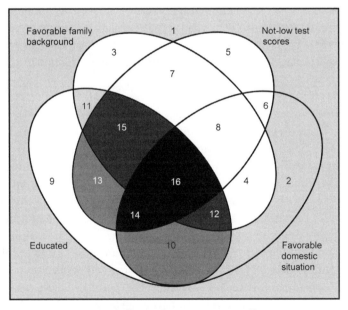

■ Subset consistency ≥ 0.90; ■ subset consistency 0.85 → 0.89; ■ subset consistency 0.80 → 0.84; ▨ subset consistency < 0.80; [ ] below frequency threshold of 1.5% of cases.

7.2. Venn diagram showing causal recipes for avoiding poverty: white female sample.

Table 7.5 Truth table results for white females not-in-poverty.

Consistency threshold	Causal recipe	Subset consistency	Outcome coverage
.90	educated•not-low-test-scores• favorable-domestic-situation	.927	.592
.85	educated•not-low-test-scores•favorable- domestic-situation + educated•not-low- test-scores•favorable-family-background + educated•favorable-family-background• favorable-domestic-situation	.927 .885 .931	.592 .625 .521
.80	educated•not-low-test-scores + educated• favorable-domestic-situation	.864 .915	.779 .618

more complex than the white male recipes. The first white male recipe combines two ingredients, *educated* and *not-low-test-scores*; white females must augment this recipe with either *favorable-domestic-situation* or *favorable-family-background* to achieve the same level of protection from poverty. Finally, for consistency ≥ .80, two two-condition recipes are derived for white females, while the white males results include a third two-condition recipe, *educated* combined with *favorable-family-background*.

Overall, the white female results, like the white male results, underscore the importance of being *educated*. The results for subset consistency ≥ .80 can be factored to show the substitutability of *not-low-test-scores* and *favorable-domestic-situation*, in combination with being *educated*:

$$educated•(not\text{-}low\text{-}test\text{-}scores + favorable\text{-}domestic\text{-}situation)$$

The subset consistency and outcome coverage scores for this solution are also very high, as they were for white males. Also like the white males, the recipes overlap considerably in their coverage of the outcome, due in part to the simple fact that 46% of white females possess all four advantages. Finally, as figure 7.2 illustrates, all the high consistency sectors are subsets of the set of *educated* respondents, just as they were for white males in figure 7.1. This figure provides graphic illustration of the centrality of education to staying out of poverty for white females. Note that of the six logically possible combinations of two advantages (using four conditions), the white female solution derived for consistency ≥ .80 lists two of the six, and both include being *educated* as a key condition. This finding indicates again that for white females the causal recipes for avoiding poverty are somewhat more limited than those for white males, which included three of the six two-advantage combinations.

Causal Recipes for Avoiding Poverty: Black Males

The results for black males contrast sharply with the results for both white males and females. It is important to note, first and foremost, that the distribution of black males in the four-dimensional vector space defined by the four fuzzy sets is very different from the distribution of whites. (See table 7.6.) For both white males and white females, the most populated sector is the one combining all four advantages, capturing 40% of white males and 46% of white females. By contrast, this sector captures only about 9% of black males. Another striking contrast: the most populated sector for black males is the combination of *educated* with *low-test-scores, unfavorable-family-background,* and *unfavorable-domestic-situation,* capturing about 22% of black males. By contrast, this sector captures only 1.2% of white females and 1% of white males (i.e., too few for the inclusion of these rows in the truth table analysis). Also, unlike whites, black males are not concentrated in a small number of sectors; thus, there are slightly more sectors (i.e., rows) that meet the frequency threshold of 1.5% of total number of cases in the sample. Only five black male rows fail to meet the frequency threshold for the truth table analysis versus seven rows each for white males and females. Together these five rows embrace less than 4% of black males.

Table 7.6 Truth table for black males showing the three outcomes.

Row #	Educated	Not-low test scores	Favorable family background	Favorable domestic situation	Number of conforming cases	Cons. ≥ .90	Cons. ≥ .85	Cons. ≥ .80
1	no	no	no	no	71	0	0	0
2	no	no	no	yes	27	0	0	0
3*	no	no	yes	no	9	-	-	-
4*	no	no	yes	yes	8	-	-	-
5	no	yes	no	no	11	0	0	0
6*	no	yes	no	yes	1	-	-	-
7*	no	yes	yes	no	3	-	-	-
8*	no	yes	yes	yes	3	-	-	-
9	yes	no	no	no	160	0	0	0
10	yes	no	no	yes	55	0	0	0
11	yes	no	yes	no	42	0	0	0
12	yes	no	yes	yes	23	0	0	0
13	yes	yes	no	no	91	0	0	0
14	yes	yes	no	yes	76	0	0	1
15	yes	yes	yes	no	80	0	1	1
16	yes	yes	yes	yes	64	1	1	1

*Indicates rows that fail to meet the frequency threshold of 1.5% of cases.

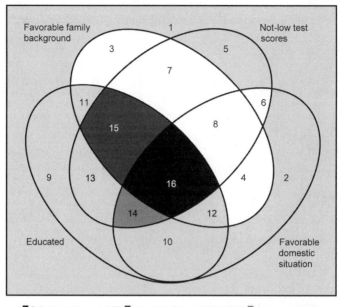

Subset consistency ≥ 0.90; ■ subset consistency 0.85 → 0.89; ■ subset consistency 0.80 → 0.84; □ subset consistency < 0.80; [ ] below frequency threshold of 1.5% of cases.

7.3 Venn diagram showing causal recipes for avoiding poverty: black male sample.

Figure 7.3 presents the four-condition Venn diagram for black males. This figure shows the combinations of conditions that are consistently linked to avoiding poverty, using the same consistency threshold values (.90, .85, and .80) and greyscale coding scheme used for whites. The black male diagram is dramatically different from the corresponding diagrams for whites. There is only one sector that meets the top consistency threshold (.90); only one sector at the next level of consistency (between .85 and .90), and only one sector at the lowest acceptable level of consistency (between .80 and .85)—a total of three consistent sectors. There are eight sectors coded light grey (consistency < .80)—indicating the combinations advantages/disadvantages that are not well insulated from poverty. The results for white males and females, by contrast, revealed only two and three light grey sectors, respectively.

Table 7.7 shows the results of the truth table analysis for black males. The top level of poverty avoidance (subset consistency ≥ .90) is reached only by black males who combine all four advantages. The next level (subset consistency ≥ .85) is achieved by black males who combine three specific advantages—being *educated* with *not-low-test-scores* and *favorable-family-*

background. Finally, at consistency ≥ .80, there are two three-advantage recipes. These two recipes can be factored to show the two common ingredients:

educated•not-low-test-scores• (favorable-family-background +
favorable-domestic-situation).

Thus, protection from poverty for black males is provided by being *educated* and having *not-low-test-scores* combined with either a favorable family background or a favorable domestic situation. These results contrast sharply with the results for whites. At consistency ≥ .80, white males had three two-advantage recipes, embracing seven sectors, while white females had two two-advantage recipes, embracing six sectors. The two three-advantage recipes shown for black males embrace only three sectors.

Several features of these results stand out. First, it is important to note the one way that the results for black males parallel the results for whites: The combinations of advantages offering the greatest protection from poverty are all subsets of *educated*. This consistent pattern underscores the importance of being *educated* to poverty avoidance, and contradicts the focus of the *Bell Curve* debate on "test scores versus family background." It is also striking to view the results for black males with respect to the contexts or conditions that enable specific causal connections. For example, under what conditions is there a link for black males between *not-low-test-scores* and poverty avoidance? The results for consistency ≥ .80 show clearly that this link occurs only when having *not-low-test-scores* is combined with being *educated* and with either a *favorable-domestic-situation* or a *favorable-family-background*. In other words, the reward for having *not-low-test-scores* occurs only in narrowly circumscribed settings. Finally, observe that the outcome coverage calculations are lower for black males than for whites. The outcome coverage scores range from .212 to .353, indicating that these conventional pathways to poverty avoidance are less commonly traveled

Table 7.7 Truth table results for black males not-in-poverty.

Consistency threshold	Causal recipe	Subset consistency	Outcome coverage
.90	educated•not-low-test-scores•favorable-family-background•favorable-domestic-situation	.896	.212
.85	educated•not-low-test-scores•favorable-family-background	.871	.272
.80	educated•not-low-test-scores•favorable-family-background + educated•not-low-test-scores•favorable-domestic-situation	.871 .842	.272 .353

by black males than by whites, due to the lower prevalence of these combinations of advantages among black males in general and the apparent
presence of alternate paths.

Causal Recipes for Avoiding Poverty: Black Females

The results for black females, like the results for black males, contrast
sharply with the results for whites. The distribution of black females in the
four-dimensional vector space defined by the four fuzzy sets is similar to
the black male distribution. Table 7.8 reveals that the sector combining
all four advantages captures only 8% of black females, compared with 9%
of black males, 40% of white males, and 46% of white females. The most
populated black female sector is the same as the most populated black male
sector—the combination of *educated* with *low-test-scores, unfavorable-family-
background,* and *unfavorable-domestic-situation,* representing about 23% of
black females. Recall that this sector represents only 1.2% of white females
and 1% of white males (i.e., too few for the inclusion of these rows in the
truth table analysis). Finally, black females are less concentrated than whites
in a small number of sectors; thus, there are more rows of the truth table
(10 for black females versus 9 each for white males and females) that pass
the frequency threshold of 1.5% of the number of cases in the sample. The

Table 7.8 Truth table for black females showing the three outcomes.

Row #	Educated	Not-low test scores	Favorable family background	Favorable domestic situation	Number of conforming cases	Cons. ≥ .90	Cons. ≥ .85	Cons. ≥ .80
1	no	no	no	no	76	0	0	0
2	no	no	no	yes	22	0	0	0
3*	no	no	yes	no	6	-	-	-
4*	no	no	yes	yes	0	-	-	-
5	no	yes	no	no	5	-	-	-
6*	no	yes	no	yes	2	-	-	-
7*	no	yes	yes	no	1	-	-	-
8*	no	yes	yes	yes	0	-	-	-
9	yes	no	no	no	180	0	0	0
10	yes	no	no	yes	87	0	0	0
11	yes	no	yes	no	39	0	0	0
12	yes	no	yes	yes	16	0	0	1
13	yes	yes	no	no	108	0	0	0
14	yes	yes	no	yes	74	0	1	1
15	yes	yes	yes	no	88	0	0	0
16	yes	yes	yes	yes	62	1	1	1

*Indicates rows that fail to meet the frequency threshold of 1.5% of cases.

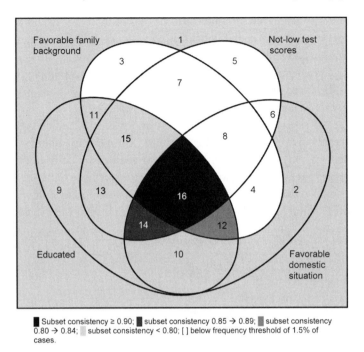

Subset consistency ≥ 0.90; ▉ subset consistency 0.85 → 0.89; subset consistency 0.80 → 0.84; subset consistency < 0.80; [ ] below frequency threshold of 1.5% of cases.

7.4. Venn diagram showing causal recipes for avoiding poverty: black female sample.

six black female rows that fail to meet the frequency threshold for the truth table analysis together embrace less than 2% of the sample. The greater distribution across rows also becomes apparent when the four samples are compared using a measure of concentration such as a Herfindahl index, defined as the sum of the squares of the proportion of respondents in a sample represented by each row of the truth table. The values of this index for black females and black males are .13 and .12, while those for white females and males are roughly twice the size at .28 and .26, suggesting again that white female and male respondents are much more concentrated in a smaller number of rows of their truth tables.

Figure 7.4 presents the four-condition Venn diagram for black females. This figure shows the combinations of conditions that are consistently linked to avoiding poverty, using the same consistency threshold values (.90, .85, and .80) and greyscale coding scheme used for the other samples. Like the black male diagram, the black female diagram is dramatically different from the corresponding diagrams for whites. Only one sector meets the top consistency threshold (.90), only one sector meets the next level of consistency (between .85 and .90), and only one sector meets the lowest acceptable level of consistency (between .80 and .85)—a total of three consistent sectors. There are seven sectors coded light grey (consistency < .80)—indicating the combinations advantages/disadvantages that are not well insulated from poverty. These results are similar to the black male results (eight light grey sectors), but very different from the results for white males and white females (with two and three light grey sectors, respectively).

Table 7.9 presents the truth table results for black females. Again, as in the results for black males, the top level of poverty avoidance (subset consistency ≥ .90) is reached only by black females who combine all four advantages. The next level (subset consistency ≥ .85) is achieved by black females who combine three specific advantages—being *educated* with *not-low-test-scores* and a *favorable-domestic-situation*. Notice that this causal recipe differs by one ingredient from the comparable recipe for black males. In place of *favorable-domestic-situation*, the comparable black male recipe lists *favorable-family-background*. Finally, at consistency ≥ .80, there are two three-advantage recipes for black females. These two recipes can be factored to show two common ingredients:

educated•favorable-domestic-situation•(not-low-test-scores +
favorable-family-background).

Again, there is an interesting contrast with the black male results: For black males, the two common ingredients were *educated* and *not-low-test-scores*. For black females, the two common ingredients are *educated* and *favorable-domestic-situation*. Thus, protection from poverty for black females is provided by being *educated* and having a *favorable-domestic-situation* combined with either *not-low-test-scores* or a *favorable-family-background*.

While similar to the results for black males, these results contrast sharply with the results for whites. At consistency ≥ .80, white males had three two-advantage recipes, embracing seven sectors, while white females had two two-advantage recipes, embracing six sectors. The two three-advantage recipes shown for black females embrace only three sectors. The result is striking: for both black males and black females, more advantages must be compounded to reach poverty avoidance levels comparable to those experienced by whites.

It is important to note several features of the results for black females. First, in common with the results for the other three samples, the combinations of advantages offering the greatest protection from poverty are all subsets of *educated*. This consistent pattern again underscores the importance of being educated to poverty avoidance. As before, it is possible to examine the contexts or conditions that enable a connection between *not-low-test-scores*

Table 7.9 Truth table results for black females not-in-poverty.

Consistency threshold	Causal recipe	Subset consistency	Outcome coverage
.90	educated•not-low-test-scores•favorable-family-background•favorable-domestic-situation	.923	.210
.85	educated•not-low-test-scores•favorable-domestic-situation	.881	.366
.80	educated•not-low-test-scores•favorable-domestic-situation + educated•favorable-family-background•favorable-domestic-situation	.881 .892	.366 .253

and poverty avoidance. The black female results for consistency ≥ .80 show clearly that this link occurs only when having *not-low-test-scores* is combined with being *educated* and a *favorable-domestic-situation*. In other words, having *not-low-test-scores* aids the struggle to avoid poverty only in a relatively narrow context. Finally, observe that the outcome coverage scores for black females are in roughly the same range as the outcome coverage scores for black males, from .210 to .366. These scores indicate that these conventional pathways to poverty avoidance are less commonly traveled by black females than by whites. More generally, the relatively modest coverage scores reflect the much lower prevalence of combinations of advantages in the black sample as well as the presence of other pathways. We examine black females' pathways to poverty in an appendix to this chapter.

Discussion

The findings presented in this chapter reveal substantial racial disparities in the connection between combinations of advantages and avoiding poverty. The paths for whites are relatively inclusive; the paths for blacks are more restrictive. These differences in causal recipes exist in tandem with the much lower prevalence of advantages in the black sample, which makes blacks doubly disadvantaged. Fewer blacks than whites are advantaged, and for blacks to avoid poverty as consistently as whites, more advantages are required.

Our results have policy implications that contrast sharply with those of both Herrnstein and Murray and Fischer et al. The policy lessons that Herrnstein and Murray derive are based on their finding that people who have low test scores, which they interpret as low cognitive ability, have a much greater risk of poverty. They assert that cognitive ability is set at birth;

thus, "for the foreseeable future, the problems of low cognitive ability are not going to be solved by outside interventions to make children smarter" (Herrnstein and Murray, 1995: 389), indicating little or no role for policy intervention aimed at addressing the causes of poverty. The simplistic policy implications of Herrnstein and Murray reflect their crude statistical model. In contrast, the policy implications of Fischer et al. are less clear-cut. Essentially, they document the effects of many different independent variables on poverty, ranging from individual-level to school-level to community-level, pointing to systems of inequality: "Family circumstances—number of siblings, parental income, cultural advantages, and so on; the quality and quantity of schooling; neighborhood conditions; job opportunities; and other features of the social context significantly boost or hold back the individual, whatever his or her talent" (Fischer et al., 1996: 204). These findings suggest that there are many different potential intervention points, with each intervention having a relatively small impact on poverty, reflecting an extensive and complex statistical model.

The policy implications of our results, by contrast, are more straightforward. First, they indicate that increasing years of completed schooling is an important foundational intervention. Every recipe for avoiding poverty includes *educated* as an ingredient. Second, our findings indicate that support for couples and for families with children is another important foundational intervention. This ingredient—*favorable-domestic-situation*—appears in more than half of the recipes for poverty avoidance. There are many couple- and family-friendly interventions that governments can implement (e.g., same-sex marriage, elimination of marriage tax penalties, affordable daycare, and so on). *Favorable-family-background* (i.e., *not-low-income-parents* combined with *not-low-parental-education*) also appears in many recipes. Unfortunately, there is little that can be done to address a causal condition that references a distant background characteristic—it is difficult to intervene in what is already set.

The same might be said of *not-low-test-scores*, that it is a distant background characteristic and therefore not subject to intervention. Herrnstein and Murray adopt this stance when they interpret test scores as a measure of inborn intelligence. It is important to note, however, that in the causal recipes we document, *not-low-test-scores* always appears in tandem with *educated*. Rather than thinking of test scores as inborn intelligence and thus as something that is causally prior to years of education, it is more realistic to see test scores as an assessment of the effectiveness of schooling. The fact that the condition *not-low-test-scores* is always accompanied by *educated* in causal recipes for avoiding poverty suggests that schooling matters more when it is effective, enabling students to achieve high scores (or at least not-low scores) on tests. It is also important to consider the fact that test scores, as a variable, brings together many different causally relevant conditions in addition to cognitive ability, such as school quality, teacher performance, home environment, family stability, physical safety, exposure to the dominant culture, situational stress, life stress, test-taking experience, test-taking anxiety, and resistance to authority, to name only a few of the factors that influence test scores. Many of these factors are school or family based and thus open to intervention.

It is important to reiterate that our results come in the form of causal recipes and not net effects. Thus, a policy of increasing years of schooling by itself would not be enough for some individuals, even though this ingredient appears in every causal recipe. For white males to achieve modest consistency in avoiding poverty (at the .80 consistency level), schooling must be combined with (1) *not-low-test-scores* (i.e., effective schooling), or (2) a *favorable-family-background* (i.e., benefits derived from the respondent's family of origin), or (3) a *favorable-domestic-situation* (i.e., having a spouse). The recipes for blacks are more complex, with each recipe embracing three ingredients at .80 consistency and four ingredients at .90 consistency.

The fact that most of the causal recipes for avoiding poverty for blacks include *favorable-family-background* as an ingredient speaks to the formidable challenge that blacks face in their efforts to avoid poverty. Consider again the racial difference in the causal recipes for the highest consistency level for poverty avoidance ($\geq$ .90). The three ingredients in the recipe for whites are *educated*, *favorable-domestic-situation*, and *not-low-test-scores*. These three ingredients, we argue, are open to policy intervention, with the emphasis given to the first two ingredients. For blacks to achieve the same level of consistency of poverty avoidance, these three ingredients must be combined with a fourth—*favorable-family-background*. Of the four ingredients we have discussed, *favorable-family-background* is the least accessible from a policy viewpoint. These results suggest that it may take generations of incremental improvements in the economic status of blacks to bring about closer racial parity in outcomes.

Appendix: Black Females in Poverty

As noted at the outset of this chapter and documented in chapter 6, there is a consistent connection between combinations of acute disadvantages and being in poverty for black females. We analyze this connection in this appendix, applying the same truth table procedure used to analyze conditions

Table 7.10 Truth table for black females in-poverty.

Row #	Not-educated	Low test scores	Unfavorable family background	Unfavorable domestic situation	Number of conforming cases	Cons. ≥ .85	Cons. ≥ .80
1	no	no	no	no	110	0	0
2	no	no	no	yes	152	0	0
3	no	no	yes	no	26	0	0
4	no	no	yes	yes	44	0	0
5	no	yes	no	no	64	0	0
6	no	yes	no	yes	127	0	0
7	no	yes	yes	no	39	0	0
8	no	yes	yes	yes	92	0	1
9*	yes	no	no	no	1	-	-
10*	yes	no	no	yes	3	-	-
11*	yes	no	yes	no	1	-	-
12*	yes	no	yes	yes	3	-	-
13*	yes	yes	no	no	8	-	-
14	yes	yes	no	yes	33	0	1
15	yes	yes	yes	no	14	0	0
16	yes	yes	yes	yes	49	1	1

*Indicates rows that fail to meet the frequency threshold of 1.5% of cases.

linked to poverty avoidance. Specifically, we examine the connections between combinations of four acute disadvantages (*not-educated*, *low-test-scores*, *unfavorable-family-background*, and *unfavorable-domestic-situation*) and being in poverty for black females. The truth table for this analysis is shown in table 7.10.[8] The distribution of respondents across the 16 combinations is uneven. Five rows have too few cases to warrant inclusion in the truth table analysis. The four most populated rows capture 63% of the respondents. About one-fourth of the black females in this sample have three or four disadvantages, but only three rows have consistent connections to poverty. One row exceeds the .85 subset consistency threshold; an additional two rows exceed the .80 subset consistency threshold.

The results of the truth table analysis are reported in table 7.11. Only two subset consistency levels are reported (.85 and .80); no truth table row had

8. The distribution of cases in this table is not the mirror of the distribution reported in table 7.8 because unfavorable-family-background is not the simple negation of favorable-family background. Using logical *and* (set intersection), unfavorable-family-background assesses the degree to which respondents combine low-parental-income with not-educated-parents, while favorable-family-background assesses the degree to which respondents combine educated-parent with not-low-parental-income. The negation of favorable-family-background is low-parental-income *or* not-educated-parents; it is not low-parental-income *and* not-educated-parents.

Table 7.11 Truth table results for black females in-poverty.

Consistency threshold	Causal recipe	Subset consistency	Outcome coverage
.85	not-educated•low-test-scores• unfavorable-family-background• unfavorable-domestic-situation	.886	.327
.80	not-educated•low-test-scores• unfavorable-domestic-situation + low-test-scores•unfavorable-family- background•unfavorable-domestic- situation	.856 .859	.399 .419

a subset consistency score ≥ .90. The higher subset consistency level (≥ .85) is found only in the row for respondents who combine all four acute disadvantages. For subset consistency ≥ .80, there are two three-condition recipes. These two recipes can be simplified by factoring the common ingredients:

$$low\text{-}test\text{-}scores \bullet unfavorable\text{-}domestic\text{-}situation \bullet (not\text{-}educated + unfavorable\text{-}family\text{-}background)$$

This factoring of the two causal recipes reveals two shared conditions— *low-test-scores* combined with an *unfavorable-domestic-situation*. These two conditions must be combined with either being *not-educated* or having an *unfavorable-family-background* to be linked to poverty. It is important to emphasize that these results are specific to black females and highlight the importance of this segment to policy makers in their efforts to address poverty, especially persistent poverty. The evidence indicates that the consequences of combined and reinforcing disadvantages are especially acute for black females.

EIGHT

Conclusion: The Black-White Gap and the Path Forward for Policy Research

Introduction

In this chapter, we revisit the main results of chapters 5–7 and offer a summary analysis that reinforces and extends our key findings. We also address the implications of the intersectional methods we present in this book for policies regarding poverty specifically and policy analysis more broadly.

The analyses we present in chapters 5–7 document consistent and substantial racial disparities. These racial disparities exist in the degree to which respondents combine advantages versus disadvantages. Racial disparities also exist in the strength of the connection between advantages and avoiding poverty and in the strength of the connection between disadvantages and experiencing poverty. The analysis of causal recipes for avoiding poverty reveals that substantial racial disparities exist in the requisite advantages. Blacks require more advantages than whites to achieve comparable levels of poverty avoidance. This finding holds at every level of consistency of poverty avoidance. Against these general findings, we now revisit the specific results of our empirical analysis before turning to a discussion of their policy implications.

Our Findings

Chapter 5. Our first analysis chapter focuses on the relationship between family background, test scores, and poverty, showing important differences between whites and blacks. More specifically, it documents very strong connections for white males and white females between both *not-low-income-parents* and *not-low-test-scores*, on the one hand, and avoiding poverty, on the other. These same connections for blacks are weaker. Furthermore, all four sets of respondents—black and white, male and female—exhibit a strong shared-outcome connection between *high-test-scores* and avoiding poverty. However, the coverage (i.e., empirical relevance) of *high-test-scores* is very low simply because of the very low prevalence of high test scores.

Parallel but slightly weaker connections exist between *high-income-parents* and avoiding poverty, with the connection again more pronounced for whites than for blacks. Blacks exhibit a strong shared-antecedent connection between both *not-high-income-parents* and *not-high-test-scores*, on the one hand, and experiencing poverty, on the other, with the two causal conditions positioned as supersets of experiencing poverty. Overall, the general pattern and most noteworthy finding is one of a strong connection between advantages and avoiding poverty for whites and a strong connection between disadvantages and experiencing poverty for blacks.

Chapter 5 also introduces the concept of *set coincidence* and demonstrates that whites have a very high coincidence of advantages—*not-low-test-scores* coincides strongly with *not-low-income-parents*. Blacks, by contrast, have a strong coincidence of disadvantages—*not-high-test-scores* coincides strongly with *not-high-income-parents*. From a set-analytic viewpoint, these results suggest that attempts to separate the effects of test scores and parental income are questionable, especially given the racial differences in patterns of set coincidence. Chapter 5 demonstrates further that the intersection of the two advantages, *not-low-test-scores* and *not-low-income-parents* performs nearly as well as these two conditions considered one at a time in accounting for poverty avoidance by whites. In parallel fashion, the intersection of the two disadvantages, *not-high-test-scores* and *not-high-income-parents*, performs nearly as well as these two conditions considered one at a time in accounting for being *in-poverty* for blacks. These results reinforce our contention that it is hazardous to try to separate the effects of these two conditions, and offer further support for our intersectional approach to the study of social inequality.

Chapter 6. Our second analysis chapter builds on chapter 5's set coincidence analysis, focusing on combinations of multiple advantages and multiple disadvantages. We first demonstrate that the coincidence of advantages is much higher for whites than for blacks, with whites registering a higher coincidence of four advantages than blacks register for two advantages. In parallel fashion, we show that the coincidence of disadvantages is much higher for blacks than for whites, with blacks registering a higher coincidence of four disadvantages than whites register for two disadvantages. We next demonstrate the divergence of correlation and set coincidence, based on an analysis of the six pairings of four conditions. Unlike correlation, set coincidence allows the separation of the analysis of coinciding advantages from the analysis of coinciding disadvantages. We show that whites' high coincidence of advantages is coupled with a low coincidence of disadvantages, while blacks' lower degree of coinciding advantages is coupled with a higher degree of coinciding disadvantages. The six pairwise correlation coefficients, by contrast, show virtually no racial differences, indicating that race-linked coincidence patterns are neutralized in correlational analyses.

Chapter 6 also examines the set-theoretic connections between combinations of advantages and avoiding poverty and between combinations of disadvantages and experiencing poverty. Altogether, five separate analyses are reported—the connections between: (1) multiple advantages and avoiding poverty, (2) multiple "exceptional" advantages and avoiding poverty, (3) multiple disadvantages and experiencing poverty, (4) multiple "acute" disadvantages and experiencing poverty, and (5) multiple disadvantages and being at risk for poverty (i.e., having membership in the set of "low-income" respondents). By far, the strongest and most consistent connection is between multiple advantages and avoiding poverty, a connection that is especially strong for whites. While subset consistency scores are higher for the connection between multiple exceptional advantages and avoiding poverty, the outcome coverage scores for exceptional advantages are low, due to the lower prevalence of exceptional advantages. With respect to the connection between acute disadvantages and being in poverty, there is consistent evidence of a connection for black females, but not for whites or for black males. Black females also exhibit a strong connection between multiple disadvantages and being at risk for poverty.

Chapter 7. Our third analysis chapter utilizes truth tables to explore the connections between different combinations of advantages and disadvantages, on the one hand, and avoiding poverty, on the other. These analyses assess the degree to which respondents with different combinations of advantages and disadvantages are included in the set of cases avoiding poverty, using three nested consistency thresholds ($\geq .80$, $\geq .85$, and $\geq .90$). Truth table analysis examines all logically possible combinations of conditions and thereby provides the foundation for identifying the specific combinations consistently linked to the outcome. Logical simplification of these combinations yields causal recipes for inclusion in the set of cases with the outcome of avoiding poverty.

We conduct separate truth table analyses for white males, white females, black males, and black females. The causal recipes for white males are very simple and broadly inclusive. Using the .80 consistency threshold yields three two-advantage recipes. The causal recipes for white females are slightly less inclusive, with two two-advantage recipes derived at .80 consistency.

Table 8.1 Summary of inclusiveness of chapter 7 recipes for avoiding poverty.

	White males	White females	Black males	Blacks females
Consistency ≥ .90	One three-advantage recipe	One three-advantage recipe	One four-advantage recipe	One four-advantage recipe
Consistency ≥ .85	One two-advantage recipe and one three-advantage recipe	Three three-advantage recipes	One three-advantage recipe	One three-advantage recipe
Consistency ≥ .80	Three two-advantage recipes	Two two-advantage recipes	Two three-advantage recipes	Two three-advantage recipes

The recipes for black males and black females are still less inclusive, with each sample displaying two three-advantage recipes. Table 8.1 summarizes the patterns documented in chapter 7 and shows that at every consistency level, the solutions for blacks are less inclusive than the solutions for whites.

The results of chapters 5–7 show consistent and dramatic racial disparities, based on comparative examination of the results of the analyses of the four race/gender samples. Our concluding analysis addresses the black-white gap directly, focusing on the size of the racial gap in consistency scores for avoiding poverty for respondents with different combinations of advantages and disadvantages.

Parsing the Racial Gap

Analyzing the conditions linked to large racial gaps in poverty avoidance is distinctly different from focusing only on the connections that are strong from a set-theoretic viewpoint, the emphasis of chapter 7. In the analysis that follows, we apply truth table techniques to the analysis of the *size of the gap* between subset consistency scores for blacks and whites. For example, suppose the subset consistency for avoiding poverty for blacks who are *educated* but have three disadvantages (*low-test-scores, unfavorable-family-background,* and *unfavorable-domestic-situation*) is .40, while the same figure for whites is .65. Neither figure approaches any of the usual thresholds for substantial subset consistency (e.g., .80); however, it is clear that the gap is substantial, and it begs analytic attention. Across the board, black subset consistency scores for avoiding poverty are less than those for whites, but there is variation in the size of the gap, ranging from substantial to small. Are there specific conditions linked to larger gaps? If, for example, large consistency gaps occur in all the rows with *"not-low-test-scores"* as a condition, the implication is clear: Blacks are not being rewarded to the same degree as whites for comparable test scores.

Another important question concerns the small consistency gaps: Are there specific conditions or combinations of conditions linked to rough racial parity? While it is true that subset consistency scores for avoiding poverty for blacks are uniformly less than those for whites, several of the gaps are small. This chapter complements the analysis of the conditions linked to large consistency gaps in poverty avoidance with an analysis of small gaps. Again, the focus of this chapter is not on which configurations are consistent subsets of the outcome, the focus of chapter 7, but on racial gaps in subset consistency scores. Using truth table techniques, it is possible to identify the causally relevant conditions linked to large gaps as well as the conditions linked to small gaps.

Table 8.2 summarizes the intersectional evidence on the racial gap in avoiding poverty. Males and females are pooled in these results, based on the finding that there are only minor gender differences within each racial sample, as documented in tables 7.2 through 7.9 and figures 7.1 through 7.4. Table 8.2 reports only the combinations of advantages/disadvantages that meet the frequency threshold of 1.5% of the respondents for *both* race samples. Altogether there are nine combinations that have sufficient numbers of both white and black respondents, using this within-sample threshold. For these nine combinations, the table reports subset consistency scores for poverty avoidance for blacks, the parallel scores for whites, and the difference between the two consistency scores—the racial gap. The combinations are sorted according to the number of advantages beginning with no advantages (i.e., four acute disadvantages) and ending with four advantages (i.e., no acute disadvantages).

The results are striking, and the pattern is clear: the fewer the advantages, the greater the racial gap. For respondents with no advantages, the subset consistency score for blacks is seventeen points lower than the white consistency score. It declines to a twelve-point gap for respondents with one or two advantages, and is only six or seven points for blacks with three advantages. For blacks with all four advantages, the gap narrows considerably, to a mere two points.

These results confirm social realities that are well-known to African-Americans—that their chances of success are comparable to whites only when they don't have any strikes against them. The greater the number of strikes, or disadvantages, the greater the racial penalty. Black respondents with the advantages that most whites possess have success rates that come very close to matching white success rates. Each additional disadvantage,

Table 8.2 Black-white consistency gap in avoiding poverty.

Educated	Not-low test scores	Favorable family background	Favorable domestic situation	Avoids poverty (blacks)	Avoids poverty (whites)	Racial gap
No advantages						
0	0	0	0	.46	.63	.17
One advantage						
0	0	0	1	.64	.76	.12
Two advantages						
1	0	0	1	.68	.81	.13
1	0	1	0	.66	.76	.10
1	1	0	0	.73	.85	.12
Three advantages						
1	0	1	1	.79	.86	.07
1	1	0	1	.84	.91	.07
1	1	1	0	.82	.88	.06
Four advantages						
1	1	1	1	.91	.93	.02

however, produces an increasing racial gap in outcomes. The four-way intersection of no advantages shows dramatic racial disparity in poverty avoidance, just as the four-way intersection of advantages reveals approximate racial parity.

Truth table analysis of large gaps. The evidence in table 8.2 can be used as a basis for a truth table analysis of the conditions linked to large racial gaps. The final column of table 8.2, the racial gap in degree of inclusion in the set of respondents avoiding poverty, is coded as an outcome in table 8.3, with the black-white consistency gap dichotomized at ten points. Gaps of at least ten points indicate a substantial racial gap in favor of whites and are coded 1; gaps of less than ten points constitute smaller racial gaps and are coded 0. The goal of the analysis is to identify the combinations of conditions that are linked to large racial gaps.

The results of the truth table analysis reveal three two-way intersections of conditions specifically linked to large racial gaps:[1]

1. These results were produced using the "intermediate" solution of fsQCA; see Ragin (2008: 164). The simplifying assumptions used here are that large racial gaps will be observed when advantages are absent. However, in this analysis the intermediate and the parsimonious solutions yield identical results.

Table 8.3 Truth table for large racial gaps in avoiding poverty.

Educated	Not-low test scores	Favorable family background	Favorable domestic situation	Racial gap	Large racial gap
0	0	0	0	.17	1
0	0	0	1	.12	1
1	0	0	1	.13	1
1	0	1	0	.10	1
1	1	0	0	.12	1
1	0	1	1	.07	0
1	1	0	1	.07	0
1	1	1	0	.06	0
1	1	1	1	.02	0

unfavorable-domestic-situation•unfavorable-family-background +
low-test-scores•unfavorable-domestic-situation +
low-test-scores•unfavorable-family-background

In other words, blacks who possess any two of the three disadvantages *unfavorable-domestic-situation, unfavorable-family-background,* and *low-test-scores* are substantially less successful than their similarly situated white counterparts in their efforts to avoid poverty. These three recipes are substitutable only as pairs of conditions, an indication of the impact of combined disadvantages for blacks and the greater gap-generating impact of additional strikes. It is important to note that this analysis pairs similarly situated blacks and whites. It reveals that specific combinations of disadvantages—*low-test-scores, unfavorable-family-background,* and *unfavorable-domestic-situation*—are more consequential for blacks than for whites when it comes to avoiding poverty. Table 8.2 shows that the weight of combined disadvantages is greater for blacks than for whites; table 8.3 pinpoints the key combinations.

Truth table analysis of small gaps. The evidence reported in table 8.3 can be reanalyzed using small gaps instead of large gaps as the focal outcome. This analysis pinpoints the combinations of advantages linked to rough racial parity in outcomes. These results, which are partially foreshadowed in table 8.2, reveal three recipes for small gaps. Each recipe combines three advantages:[2]

---

2. These results were also produced using the "intermediate" solution; the simplifying assumption is that a small racial gap will be observed when advantages are present.

educated•favorable-domestic-situation•favorable-family-background +
educated•not-low-test-scores•favorable-domestic-situation +
educated•not-low-test-scores•favorable-family-background.

These recipes can be factored, as follows, to highlight the common ingredient, *educated*:

educated•(favorable-domestic-situation•favorable-family-background +
not-low-test-scores•favorable-domestic-situation +
not-low-test-scores•favorable-family-background).

In short, when being *educated* is combined with any two of the three advantages *not-low-test-scores, favorable-family-background,* or *favorable-domestic-situation,* the gap between blacks and whites is smaller. These findings reinforce our initial observation that the fewer the disadvantages, the smaller the gap, and they complement one of the key findings of chapter 7—the importance of education as a key ingredient. Not only is education central to efforts to avoid poverty, it is also consistently linked, in conjunction with other advantages, to greater racial parity in poverty avoidance.

Revisiting the *Bell Curve* Debate

Summarizing the results of their analysis, Herrnstein and Murray argue that if a person could choose between being born into a high SES (socioeconomic status) family and being born with a high level of "intelligence," she would be much better off choosing "intelligence" (Herrnstein and Murray, 1994:127). They base this conclusion on the stronger net effect of AFQT scores compared to parental SES on life outcomes such as poverty. The imagery of "choosing" is closely linked to the analytic premise that causal variables have independent effects and that the separate impact of each variable on an outcome can be validly estimated. Fischer et al. criticize Herrnstein and Murray's conclusions, but do not challenge this analytic premise. They ground their critique in a thorough reanalysis of the *Bell Curve* data, utilizing the same logistic regression technique used by Herrnstein and Murray, while radically augmenting the number of competing independent variables. In the end, they acknowledge that the test score variable has a significant effect on poverty, but argue that it is not nearly as strong or as important as Herrnstein and Murray claim.

The set coincidence analyses we present show clearly that, for whites, choosing either *not-low-parental-income* or *not-low-test-scores* usually involves choosing the other. As sets, the two conditions overlap considerably. While no one would "choose" to have *not-high-parental-income* or *not-high-test-scores*, these two attributes are closely coupled in the black sample. The set coincidence scores are very high, so much so that the fundamental approach of calculating the "net effect" of either test scores or parental income, as both Herrnstein and Murray and Fischer et al. attempt, seems highly questionable from a set-analytic perspective. Furthermore, the racial difference in the patterns of overlap makes such assessments especially problematic. We show further that it is not simply the overlap of test scores and parental income that is at issue. Advantages, in general, substantially overlap for whites, while disadvantages, in general, substantially overlap for blacks. Herrnstein and Murray's fiction of "choosing intelligence" is an inviting and seductive thought experiment; however, it has little relevance to the reality of overlapping and reinforcing advantages and disadvantages—constitutive features of social inequality in the U.S. today.

The striking racial differences in coinciding advantages versus disadvantages by race are invisible to correlational and net effects analysis. The logistic regression results presented in chapter 3 and the correlational analysis presented in chapter 6 in fact show quite similar results across race/gender samples. While consistent with the results of both Herrnstein and Murray and Fischer et al., this uniformity across race samples contradicts both everyday experience and our set coincidence analyses. It may seem that set coincidence and correlation results should parallel each other; however, they do not for two important reasons: (1) As noted previously, correlation is symmetric by design, while set coincidence is asymmetric by design, and (2) correlation is expressed in standardized scores and is thus metric neutral, while set coincidence is a proportion (set intersection as a proportion of set union) and thus has a fixed and directly interpretable metric.

The importance of coinciding advantages is clearly visible in the strong connection between combinations of advantages and avoiding poverty: The greater the number of coinciding advantages, the greater the consistency of poverty avoidance (chapter 6), especially for whites. Blacks must accumulate more advantages than whites in order to secure comparable outcomes (chapter 7). The fewer the advantages, the larger the racial gap in outcomes (this chapter). These findings contrast sharply with the emphasis of both Herrnstein and Murray and Fischer et al. Both research teams attempt to estimate the unvarnished "true" effect of test scores, purging from these estimates the confounding effects of competing variables (e.g., parental SES). While deriving trustworthy estimates of the net effect of test scores is a worthwhile endeavor, our results strongly indicate that test scores impact poverty *in combination* with other causally relevant conditions, and not as an "independent" variable.

Beyond Conventional Policy Research

A central goal of this work has been to present an alternative to conventional approaches to the analysis of policy-relevant data. As we have argued, the customary focus on net effects of independent variables and the use of correlation-based methods tend to hide from view the intersectional nature of social inequality. Instead, the set-analytic approach we offer shifts the focus from the separate effects of independent variables to "causal recipes," asking "What *combinations* of causally relevant conditions are linked to the avoidance versus the experience of poverty?" Our approach reflects the fundamentally intersectional nature of social inequality—a quality that is relevant to the analysis of many social and "wicked" problems, beyond poverty. It is this quality that makes the application of a set-theoretic approach so powerful (Blackman, Wistow, and Byrne, 2013).

The first and in many ways the most important contribution we seek to make is to shift scholarly attention to how advantages and disadvantages combine and intersect in their impact on policy-relevant outcomes such as poverty. While our contribution is grounded in a methodology that focuses on set-theoretic analysis, the shift we propose is not merely one of methodology, but more fundamentally, specific to the way social scientists approach the study of intersectional phenomena such as poverty. The tools that we, as social scientists, use to examine policy-relevant data significantly shape both our understanding of the phenomena and the way the debate over them unfolds. The standard tools of multivariate analysis—starting with their implicit assumption of a contest between variables to explain variation in an outcome—tend to reflect and reinforce the ideological contest between political camps, as witnessed in the debate over the *Bell Curve*. But the problems run even deeper. The standard correlational tools focus on estimating a "correct" average treatment effect across a range of diverse cases. This is an important task; however, we argue that it does not necessarily provide the empirical insights that are most helpful to policymakers, who often are looking for more nuanced insights.

Consider again the policy advice that emerged from the *Bell Curve* debate. On the one hand, the underspecified model of Herrnstein and Murray (1994:135) offered relatively blunt advice in suggesting that "cognitive ability is more important than parental SES in determining poverty." In their view, cognitive ability is essentially fixed at birth; thus, the role of policy intervention is correspondingly limited. On the other hand, the overspecified model of Fischer et al. pointed to a variety of factors at the individual, school, and community level, but offered little specific policy guidance. Each potential intervention is likely to have only a relatively small impact on reducing poverty. While we agree with Fischer et al.'s (1996:205) emphasis on "systems of inequality," the methodologically orthodox approach they use does not take into account the intersectional nature of such systems.

In contrast, we believe that the set-analytic methods we advocate are powerful tools for policy-relevant analysis precisely because they are built on the assumption of intersecting inequalities and can be used to aid the identification of context-specific interventions. Instead of focusing on the average treatment effect across a population, the methods we propose allow researchers to determine under what conditions a specific intervention may be effective. Our point is that policymakers frequently are interested in remedying the plight of especially hard-hit segments of a population and are often less concerned about the average effects of causal variables. Consider, for example, the debate over welfare reform in the United States (e.g., Harris, 1996; Rose, 2000; Lichter and Jayakody, 2002). Much of the focus was on the reform's impact on low-income single mothers. When targeting specific population segments, the set-analytic methods demonstrated here offer much greater insight into the type of intervention that may be appropriate in a given context.

Before examining specific policy-relevant insights that follow from our study, it is important to be clear about its limitations. To be sure, any insight that might be gained is limited to the patterns that can be extracted from the survey data we use. By revisiting one of the most heated debates over the causes of poverty, we are able to apply our methods to one of the most analyzed datasets in the social sciences and also to contrast our findings with those of two opposing camps. However, this strategy also has several limitations.

First, the data, while extensive, are by now somewhat dated, as the outcome was measured in 1990. One might argue that the fundamental processes of intersectionality we document are likely to be quite durable (see, e.g., Tilly, 1999) and that the general patterns are very likely to be the same today. But the fact remains that our data are not current and thus limit our ability to speak to specific policy choices today.

Second, our analyses do not address important concerns that have surfaced in the literature on poverty, namely the role of geographic and cultural factors. For instance, there is now a significant literature on patterns

of urban poverty (Small and Newman, 2001) that has shifted attention towards cultural and neighborhood explanations of inequality (e.g., Massey
and Denton, 1993; Corcoran, 1995; Wilson, 1996; Lamont, 1999). While
these are important concerns, we cannot address them due to the limitations of our data.[3]

Third, while the set-theoretic methods we use are directly aligned with
the intersectional nature of advantages and disadvantages, they are not capable of supplanting the deeply textured knowledge of the causes of poverty
offered by qualitative researchers (e.g., Edin and Lein, 1997; Kaplan, 1997;
Edin and Kefalas, 2005). While we affirm that causality is most accessible
through rich qualitative work, it is the combination of such insights with
intersectional analyses such as the one we offer in this work that in our view
provides the most promising way forward.

These limitations indicate that our analysis first and foremost has implications for "how" to do policy-relevant research rather than "what" policy
makers should do based on our specific findings. Thus, we need to be cau-
tious in offering recommendations. The insights we offer are relatively high
level and do not speak to the specific features of existing policies. On that
note, we review the major empirical insights that follow from our analyses.

Racial disparities in patterns of poverty avoidance. A key finding in the
analyses of Herrnstein and Murray and those of Fischer et al. is that there
are very few differences across subgroups in terms of which independent
variables have statistically significant effects. In fact, the results for whites
and blacks are very similar regarding what appears to matter most, and the
picture that emerges is one of very little racial difference in causal patterns.
However, when viewed through the lens of the set-analytic methods we employ here, it is clear that there are striking differences in how blacks and
whites are able to avoid poverty. Whites have more paths to avoiding poverty, and the paths are relatively inclusive, meaning they require fewer combined advantages in order to avoid poverty. By contrast, blacks have fewer
paths to avoiding poverty and the paths are more restrictive. For example,
while whites are consistently able to avoid poverty by simply combining being *educated* with *not-low test scores*, this is not the case for blacks.

---

3. Another data limitation is that we focus primarily on money income, which excludes
noncash benefits and refundable tax credits. Insofar as these noncash benefits have grown more
rapidly in the past decades (Danziger and Wimer, 2014), their influence would not be reflected
here. Similarly, to maintain comparability with the prior contributions to the *Bell Curve* debate,
we did not use alternate measures of poverty such as the Supplementary Poverty Measure now
used by the Census Bureau.

Racial disparities in combinations of advantages versus disadvantages. A second key pattern that is invisible to the correlational analyses of both Herrnstein and Murray and Fischer et al. relates to the substantial racial differences in combinations of advantages versus disadvantages and their different connections to experiencing versus avoiding poverty. As we have noted, because correlational analysis is symmetric, it is largely blind to the differences between the conditions linked to the presence of an outcome such as poverty and the conditions linked to its absence. In contrast, by analyzing poverty and its avoidance separately and further calibrating our causal conditions in terms of advantages and disadvantages we are able to demonstrate striking racial differences in coinciding advantages versus disadvantages.

To begin, there is a fundamental difference in the distribution of black and white respondents across combinations of advantages and disadvantages. For whites, the most populated sector is the one combining all four advantages (*educated, not-low-test-scores, favorable-family-background, favorable-domestic-situation*), which accounts for 40% of white males and 46% of white females. By contrast, only 9% of black males and 8% of black females combine all four advantages. Regarding combinations of disadvantages, our findings indicate again a major racial disparity. The most populated sector for blacks is the combination of *educated* with three disadvantages (*low-test-scores, unfavorable-family-background, unfavorable-domestic-situation*), which accounts for 22% of black males and 23% of black females. By contrast, this same combination captures less than 1.5% of white males and females—too few, in fact, to allow a robust set-theoretic analysis of these combinations. What emerges is thus a picture where whites tend to enjoy compound advantages while blacks tend to experience compound disadvantages. These findings speak to the growing realization that there are significant racial disparities in earnings that contradict simple accounts of a black-white wage gap (Grodsky and Pager, 2001), suggesting that "group gaps do not mean the same thing, nor are they the same size, at different locations in the earnings distribution. The mechanisms that produce them (and, presumably, the policies that will close them) differ as well" (Leicht, 2008: 242).

This fundamental racial disparity in intersecting advantages and disadvantages carries over into how they are connected to avoiding versus experiencing poverty. Blacks must accumulate more advantages to avoid poverty to the same degree as whites. While blacks with all four advantages are similar to whites in that both groups tend to consistently avoid poverty, the racial gap increases as the number of advantages decreases. Further, our findings indicate that black females are distinct from the other three samples in that they are the only group to show a consistent link between combinations of disadvantages and being in poverty. Our findings thus demonstrate that the consequences of combined and reinforcing disadvantages are especially acute for black females. Again, this finding is largely hidden from correlational analyses, which may explain a pattern noted by Browne and Misra: Prior qualitative research has suggested a clear pattern of intersectionality of race and gender, while large-scale quantitative studies (e.g., of wage inequality) have largely failed to find intersectionality and instead have suggested that race and gender are largely independent factors of inequality.

Finally, the intersectional nature of our analyses allows us to compare the impact of combined advantages versus combined disadvantages. Regarding the question as to which are stronger—combined advantages or combined disadvantages—the answer appears to be that combined advantages are more consistently linked to being out of poverty than combined disadvantages are linked to the experience of poverty.

The interdependence of advantages. Another key insight that emerges from our analysis is the interdependent nature of how advantages aid the avoidance of poverty, a finding that again highlights the intersectional nature of social inequality. Consider for instance the impact of *favorable-family-background*. Having this advantage offers protection from poverty only when it is combined with being *educated*, often along with other advantages. By itself it does not consistently protect individuals from poverty. This finding contradicts sharply with the focus on net effects that dominates the analyses of both Herrnstein and Murray and Fischer et al. The same is true of test scores. It is evident that having *not-low-test-scores* matters only when combined with other causal conditions such as being *educated* and having a *favorable-domestic-situation*. This indicates that having *not-low-test-scores* aids the struggle to avoid poverty only in relatively circumscribed contexts.

The implications of our findings also speak to the literature on cumulative advantage. In this regard, Lin and Harris have suggested that it is primarily cumulative disadvantages that reinforce each other, while "by contrast, advantages insulate. Being affluent does not guarantee parental attention, good behavior, academic support, or friends of good character. Doing well in school does not prevent job loss or guarantee a successful marriage. The presence of enough advantages, however, makes it easier to cushion the negative impact of single disadvantages" (Lin and Harris, 2010: 3). Our findings lead to a different insight more in line with prior work on cumulative advantage (e.g. Merton, 1968; DiPrete and Eirich, 2006), which indicates that advantages not only cushion the impact of single disadvantages, but also combine synergistically to protect individuals from the risk of poverty.

The central role of education. While blacks and whites show very important differences in the intersectionality of their advantages and disadvantages, there are also some commonalities in their experiences. Perhaps the most striking finding of our set-analytic approach concerns the key role that education plays in the avoidance of poverty. Being educated is part of every causal recipe for avoiding poverty. Our findings indicate that increasing the years of completed schooling is a foundational intervention that should be part of policies aimed at reducing poverty. Prior literature has, of course, noted that a lack of education presents a key barrier to advancement (e.g., Lichter and Jayakody, 2002; Danziger, 2010). What our analysis adds is a demonstration of the pervasiveness of education to the avoidance of poverty.

It is important to note that education presents to some extent a "positional" advantage. While human capital arguments indicate that educational qualifications provide skills and knowledge that, via participation in the labor market, can help reduce the likelihood of poverty, the value of such qualifications depends partly on the qualifications held by others. This feature makes educational attainment different from, for instance, having a favorable domestic situation, which would appear to present an absolute rather than relative advantage. From a policy point of view, this suggests that it is important to raise the level of those most likely to suffer poverty independently of any general rise in levels or qualifications, as indicated, for example, by the growing college/noncollege wage gap (e.g., Morris and Western, 1999; Leicht, 2008; McCall, 2000).

The importance of a favorable domestic situation. Finally, our findings point to the role of having a favorable domestic situation in the effort to avoid poverty. This factor appears in more than half of all causal recipes for avoiding poverty, a finding that holds for both blacks and whites and is in line with the position that family structure plays a significant role in the avoidance of poverty (e.g., Massey, 2007; McLanahan and Percheski, 2008). This finding suggests that, along with additional years of education, the second most important intervention should focus on aiding couples and parents. As we have pointed out, there are a number of couple- and family-friendly interventions that could be implemented, such as same-sex marriage, the elimination of marriage tax penalties, the provision of subsidized or otherwise more affordable daycare, and so on.

Conclusion

We began this book with the methodological premise that social inequality is best viewed and studied intersectionally and that set-analytic methods are especially well-suited for intersectional analysis. Taking this as a starting point, our goal has been to examine how different advantages and disadvantages coincide, how patterns of intersection vary across both race and gender, and how the coincidence of advantages versus disadvantages impacts life chances. Using set-analytic methods, we have demonstrated that intersecting inequalities are at the root of racial disparities in poverty. The implication of Herrnstein and Murray's championing of test scores as the master cause is that the black-white gap in test scores "explains" the black-white gap in poverty. Our research challenges this simple-minded view. The answer to the question "What matters more, family background or test scores?" is that these and other inequalities are interwoven into the fabric of social life, which means, in turn, that they are best studied intersectionally. As social scientists, our task is to identify consequential intersections and document their impact, not to choose sides in ideological debates by willfully magnifying or undermining the importance of favorite "independent" variables.

A central theme of our approach has been the idea that advantages and disadvantages are cumulative and that they reinforce each other. The idea that disadvantages especially compound and interlock resonates with the stubborn persistence of poverty and has a depressing corollary, namely, that it will be more difficult to reduce poverty if its causes are intertwined and cumulative in nature. In a sense, it would be much easier if we lived in a world where the essential question was simply "what matters most?" As Lin and Harris (2010) note, however, the search for magic bullets has resulted in piecemeal approaches to poverty, with researchers seeking to identify the single determinant of economic success that would then resolve the host of economic, cultural, and social problems associated with poverty. It is not surprising that given the inherently intersectional nature of inequality, such searches are unlikely to yield the desired results. Like Lin and Harris, we believe that "our policies need to be explicit in confronting race and holistic in their scope" (2010:16). We believe that the approach we advocate in this work is well-equipped to contribute to just such policies.

BIBLIOGRAPHY

Blackman, Tim, Jonathan Wistow, and Dave Byrne. 2013. Using Qualitative Comparative Analysis to Understand Complex Policy Problems. Evaluation, 19: 126–140.

Browne, Irene, and Joya Misra. 2003. The Intersection of Gender and Race in the Labor Market. Annual Review of Sociology, 29: 487–513.

Byrne, David and Charles C. Ragin (eds.). 2009. The Sage Handbook of Case-Based Methods. Thousand Oaks, CA: Sage.

Carmines, Edward G., and Richard A. Zeller. 1979. Reliability and Validity Assessment. Quantitative Applications in the Social Sciences, no. 17. Thousand Oaks: Sage.

Cavallo, Alexander, Hazem El-Abbadi, and Randal Heeb. 1997. The Hidden Gender Restriction: The Need for Proper Controls When Testing for Racial Discrimination. In Intelligence and Success: Scientists Respond to *The Bell Curve*, edited by Bernie Devlin, Stephen Fienberg, Daniel Resnick, and Kathryn Roeder, pp. 193–214. New York: Springer Verlag.

Cawley, John, Karen Conneely, James Heckman, and Edward Vytlacil. 1997. Cognitive Ability, Wages, and Meritocracy. In Intelligence, Genes, and Success: Scientists Respond to *The Bell Curve*, edited by Bernie Devlin, Stephen E. Fienberg, Daniel P. Resnick, and Kathryn Roeder, 179–192. New York: Springer.

Choo, Hae Yeon, and Myra Marx Ferree. 2010. Practicing Intersectionality in Sociological Research: A Critical Analysis of Inclusions, Interactions, and Institutions in the Study of Inequalities. Sociological Theory, 28(2): 129–149.

Chuang, Hwei-Lin. 1990. Descriptions for the School Array and Highest Grade Completed Array. Draft Notes, CHRR, Ohio State University, 1990.

Collins, Patricia Hill. 2015. Intersectionality's Definitional Dilemmas. Annual Review of Sociology, 41: 1–20.

Corcoran, Mary. 1995. Rags to Rags: Poverty and Mobility in the United States. Annual Review of Sociology, 21: 237–267.

Crenshaw, Kimberlé. 1989. Demarginalizing the Intersection of Race and Sex: A Black Feminist Critique of Antidiscrimination Doctrine, Feminist Theory, and Antiracist Politics. University of Chicago Legal Forum 1989: 139–167.

Crenshaw, Kimberlé. 1991. Mapping the Margins: Intersectionality, Identity Politics, and Violence against Women of Color. Stanford Law Review 43(6): 1241–1279.

Danziger, Sandra K. 2010. The Decline of Cash Welfare and Implications for Social Policy and Poverty. Annual Review of Sociology, 36: 523–545.

Danziger, Sheldon, and Christopher Wimer. 2014. Poverty. In State of the Union: The Poverty and Inequality Report, pp. 13–18. Special Issue of Pathways Magazine: A Magazine on Poverty, Inequality, and Social Policy. Stanford, CA: Stanford Center on Poverty and Inequality.

Davis, Kathy. 2008. Intersectionality as Bbuzzword: A Sociology of Science Perspective on What Makes a Feminist Theory Successful. Feminist Theory, 9(1): 67–85.

Dawes, Robyn M. 1978. The Robust Beauty of Improper Linear Models in Decision Making. American Psychologist, 34(7): 571–582.

Devlin, Bernie, Stephen E. Fienberg, Daniel P. Resnick, and Kathryn Roeder. 1997. Intelligence, Genes, and Success: Scientists Respond to The Bell Curve. New York: Copernicus.

Dickens, William T., Thomas Kane, and Charles Schultze. 1997. Does the Bell Curve Ring True? A Reconsideration. Washington, DC: Brookings Institution.

DiPrete, Thomas A., and Gregory M. Eirich. 2006. Cumulative Advantage as a Mechanism for Inequality: A Review of Theoretical and Empirical Developments. Annual Review of Sociology, 32: 271–297.

Duncan, Greg J., and Willard L. Rodgers. 1988. Longitudinal Aspects of Childhood Poverty. Journal of Marriage and Family, 50(4): 1007–1021.

Duncan, Greg J., Bjorn Gustafsson, Richard Hauser, Gunther Schmaus, Stephen Jenkins, Hans Messinger, Ruud Muffels, Brian Nolan, Jean-Claude Ray, and Wolfgang Voges. 1995. Poverty and Social-Assistance Dynamics in the United States, Canada, and Europe. in Poverty, Inequality, and the Future of Social Policy: Western States and the New World Order, pp. 67–108. New York: Russell Sage Foundation.

Edin, Kathryn, and Maria Kefalas. 2005. Promises I Can Keep: Why Poor Women Put Motherhood before Marriage. Berkeley: University of California Press.

Edin, Kathryn, and Laura Lein. 1997. Making Ends Meet: How Single Mothers Survive Welfare and Low Wage Work. New York: Russell Sage Foundation.

Fischer, Claude S., Michael Hout, Martín Sánchez Jankowski, Samuel R. Lucas, Ann Swidler, and Kim Voss. 1996. Inequality by Design: Cracking the Bell Curve Myth. Princeton: Princeton University Press.

Fraser, Steve. 1995. The Bell Curve Wars: Race, Intelligence, and the Future of America. New York: BasicBooks.

Glaesser, Judith, and Barry Cooper. 2012a. Educational Achievement in Selective and Comprehensive Local Education Authorities: A Configurational Analysis. British Journal of Sociology of Education, 33: 223–244.

Glaesser, Judith, and Barry Cooper. 2012b. Gender, Parental Education, and Ability: Their Interacting Roles in Predicting GCSE Success. Cambridge Journal of Education, 42: 463–480.

Grodsky, Eric, and Devah Pager. 2001. The Structure of Disadvantage: Individual and Occupational Determinants of the Black-White Wage Gap. American Sociological Review, 66: 542–567.

Gross, Alan. 1981. An Optimal Property of Least Squares Weights in Prediction Models. Psychometrika, 46(2): 161–169.

Hancock, Ange-Marie. 2007a. Intersectionality as a Normative and Empirical Paradigm. Politics & Gender, 3(2): 248–254.

Hancock, Ange-Marie. 2007b. When Multiplication Doesn't Equal Quick Addition: Examining Intersectionality as a Research Paradigm. Perspectives on Politics 5 (1): 63–79.

Hancock, Ange-Marie. 2013. Empirical Intersectionality: A Tale of Two Approaches. U.C. Irvine Law Review, 3: 259–296.

Hankivsky, Olena, and Renee Cormier. 2011. Intersectionality and Public Policy: Some Lessons from Existing Models. Political Research Quarterly, 64 (1): 217–229.

Harris, Kathleen Mullan. 1996. Life after Welfare: Women, Work, and Repeat Dependency. American Sociological Review, 61(3): 407–426.

Heckman, James J. 1995. Cracked Bell (review of The Bell Curve). Reason 26(March): 49–56.

Herrnstein, Richard J., and Charles A. Murray. 1994. The Bell Curve: Intelligence and Class Structure in American Life. New York: Free Press.

Hudson , John, and Stefan Kühner. 2013. Qualitative Comparative Analysis and Applied Public Policy Analysis: New Applications of Innovative Methods. Policy and Society, 32: 279–287.

Jacoby, Russell, Naomi Glauberman, and Richard J. Herrnstein. 1995. The Bell Curve Debate: History, Documents, Opinions. New York: Times Books.

Jencks, Christopher, and Susan E. Mayer. 1990. The Social Consequences of Growing Up in a Poor Neighborhood. In Inner-City Poverty in the United States, ed. J. L. Lynn and M. G. H. McGreary, pp. 111–186. Washington, DC: National Academy.

Jencks, Christopher, and Meredith Phillips (eds.). 1998. The Black-White Test Score Gap. Washington, DC: Brookings Institute.

Kaplan, Elaine Bell. 1997. Not Our Kind of Girl: Unraveling the Myths of Black Teenage Motherhood. Berkeley: University of California Press.

Kincheloe, Joe L., Shirley R. Steinberg, and Aaron David Gresson. 1996. Measured Lies: The Bell Curve Examined. New York: St. Martin's Press.

Lahn, B.T. and L. Ebenstein. 2009. Let's Celebrate Human Genetic Diversity. Nature 461(7265): 726–728.

Lamont, Michelle. 1999. The Cultural Territories of Race: Black and White Boundaries. Chicago: University of Chicago Press; New York: Russel Sage Foundation.

Levine, David I., and Gary Painter. 1998. The NELS Curve: Replicating The Bell Curve. Berkeley: Institute for Research on Labor and Employment.

Leicht, Kevin T. 2008. Broken Down by Race and Gender? Sociological Explanations of New Sources of Earnings Inequality. Annual Review of Sociology, 34: 237–255.

Leicht, Kevin T., and Scott T. Fitzgerald. 2006. Post-Industrial Peasants: The Illusion of Middle Class Prosperity. New York: Worth.

Lichter, Daniel T. 1997. Poverty and Inequality among Children. Annual Review of Sociology, 23:121–145.

Lichter, Daniel T., and Rukamalie Jayakody. 2002. Welfare Reform: How Do We Measure Success? Annual Review of Sociology, 28: 117–141.

Lin, Ann Chih, and David R. Harris (eds.). 2008. The Colors of Poverty: Why Racial and Ethnic Disparities Persist (National Poverty Center Series on Poverty and Public Policy). New York: Russel Sage Foundation.

Little, Roderick J. A., and Donald B. Rubin. 1987. Statistical Analysis with Missing Data. New York: John Wiley & Sons.

Manolakes, L. A. 1997. Cognitive Ability, Environmental Factors, and Crime: Predicting Frequent Criminal Activity. In Intelligence, Genes, and Success: Scientists Respond to The Bell Curve, edited by Bernie Devlin, Stephen E. Fienberg, Daniel P. Resnick, and Kathryn Roeder, 235–255. New York: Springer-Verlag.

Massey, Douglas S. 2007. Catgorically Unequal: The American Stratification System. New York: Russel Sage Foundation.

Massey, Douglas S., and Nancy A. Denton. 1993. American Apartheid: Segregation and the Making of the Underclass. Cambridge, MA: Harvard University Press.

McCall, Leslie. 2000. Gender and the New Inequality: Explaining the College/Noncollege Wage Gap. American Sociological Review, 65: 234–265.

McCall, Leslie. 2005. The Complexity of Intersectionality. Signs: Journal of Women in Culture and Society, 30(2): 1771–1800.

McCall, Leslie, and Christine Percheski. 2010. Income Inequality: New Trends and Research Directions. Annual Review of Sociology, 36: 329–347.

McLanahan, Sara, and Christine Percheski. 2008. Family Structure and the Reproduction of Inequalities. Annual Review of Sociology, 34: 257–258.

Merton, Robert K. 1968. The Matthew Effect in Science: The reward and Communication Systems of Science Are Considered. Science, 159: 56–63.

Moffitt, Robert A. 1998. The Effect of Welfare on Marriage and Fertility. In Welfare, the Family, and Reproductive Behavior, edited by Robert Moffitt, pp. 50–97. Washington DC: National Academy Press.

Morris, Martina, and Bruce Western. 1999. Inequality in Earnings at the Close of the Twentieth Century. Annual Review of Sociology, 25: 623–657.

Nash, Jennifer C. 2008. Re-thinking Intersectionality. Feminist Review, 89: 1–15.

National Research Council. 1996. Measuring Poverty: A New Approach. Washington, DC: National Academy of Science Press.

Neckerman, Kathryn M., and Florencia Torche. 2007. Inequality: Causes and Consequences. Annual Review of Sociology, 33: 335–357.

Neff, Daniel. 2013. Fuzzy Set Theoretic Applications in Poverty Research. Policy and Society, 32: 319–331.

Nisbett, Richard E. 1998. Race, Genetics, and IQ. In The Black-White Test Score Gap, edited by C. Jencks and M. Phillips, pp. 86–102. Washington, DC: Brookings Institution Press.

NLSY79 User's Guide. 1999. A Guide to the 1979–1998 National Longitudinal Survey of Youth Data. Columbus: Center for Human Resource Research, Ohio State University.

Nolan, Brian, and Christopher T. Whelan. 1999. Loading the Dice? A Study of Cumulative Disadvantage. Dublin: Oak Tree Press.

Pattillo-McCoy, Mary. 1999 Black Picket Fences: Privilege and Peril among the Black Middle Class. Chicago: University of Chicago Press.

Phillips, M., J. Brooks-Gunn, G. J. Duncan, P. K. Klebanov, and J. Crane. 1998. Family Background, Parenting Practices, and the Black–White Test Score Gap. In the Black-White Test Score Gap, edited by C. Jencks and M. Phillips, pp. 102–145. Washington, DC: Brookings Institution Press.

Ragin, Charles C. 1987. The Comparative Method: Moving beyond Qualitative and Quantitative Strategies, Berkeley: University of California Press.

Ragin, Charles C. 1994. Constructing Social Research: The Unity and Diversity of Method. Thousand Oaks, CA: Pine Forge Press.

Ragin, Charles C. 2000. Fuzzy-Set Social Science. Chicago: University of Chicago Press.

Ragin, Charles C. 2008. Redesigning Social Inquiry: Fuzzy Sets and Beyond. Berkeley: University of California Press.

Ragin, Charles C., and Lisa M. Amoroso. 2011. Constructing Social Research: The Unity and Diversity of Method, 2nd ed. Thousand Oaks, CA: Pine Forge Press.

Ragin, Charles C., and Howard S. Becker (eds). 1992. What Is a Case? Exploring the Foundations of Social Inquiry. Cambridge: Cambridge University Press.

Rihoux, Benoît, and Heike Grimm (eds.). 2006. Innovative Comparative Methods for Policy Analysis. New York: Springer.

Rose, Nancy E. 2000. Scapegoating Poor Women: An Analysis of Welfare Reform. Journal of Economic Issues, 34(1): 143–57.

Small, Mario Luis, and Katherine Newman. 2001. Urban Poverty after *The Truly Disadvantaged*: The Rediscovery of the Family, the Neighborhood, and Culture. Annual Review of Sociology, 27: 23–45.

Social Security Administration. 1998. Bulletin. Annual Statistical Supplement. Office of Policy. Office of Research, Evaluation, and Statistics.

Thompson, Jeffrey, and Timothy Smeeding. 2014. Income Inequality. In State of the Union: The Poverty and Inequality Report, pp. 28–33. Special Issue of Pathways Magazine: A Magazine on Poverty, Inequality, and Social Policy. Stanford, CA: Stanford Center on Poverty and Inequality.

Tilly, Charles. 1999. Durable Inequality. Berkeley: University of California Press.

Varner, Charles, Marybeth Mattingly, and David Grusky. 2014. Executive Summary. In State of the Union: The Poverty and Inequality Report, pp. 3–7. Special Issue of Pathways Magazine: A Magazine on Poverty, Inequality, and Social Policy. Stanford, CA: Stanford Center on Poverty and Inequality.

Wainer, Howard. 1976. Estimating Coefficients in Linear Models: It Don't Make No Nevermind. Psychological Bulletin, 83(2): 213–217.

Wainer, Howard. 1978. On the Sensitivity of Regression and Regressors. Psychological Bulletin, 85(2): 267–273.

Walby, Sylvia, Jo Armstrong, and Sofia Strid. 2012. Intersectionality: Multiple Inequalities in Social Theory. Sociology 46(2): 224–240.

Wiggins, Nancy, and Eileen S. Kohen. Man versus Model of Man Revisited. Journal of Personality and Social Psychology, 19: 10–106.

Wilson, William J. 1996. When Work Disappears: The World of the New Urban Poor. New York: Knopf.

Winship, Christopher, and Sanders Korenman. 1997. Does Staying in School Make You Smarter? The Effect of Education on IQ in *The Bell Curve*. In Intelligence, Genes, and Success: Scientists respond to *The Bell Curve*, edited by Bernie Devlin, Stephen E. Fienberg, Daniel P. Resnick, and Kathryn Roeder, pp. 215–234. New York: Springer.

INDEX